# Quilted Havens

## CITY HOUSES, COUNTRY HOMES

Susan Purney-Mark & Daphne Greig

**American Quilter's Society**

P. O. Box 3290 • Paducah, KY 42002-3290
e-mail: AQSquilt@apex.net

Located in Paducah, Kentucky, the American Quilter's Society (AQS) is dedicated to promoting the accomplishments of today's quilters. Through its publications and events, AQS strives to honor today's quiltmakers and their work and to inspire future creativity and innovation in quiltmaking.

EDITOR: MARY JO KURTEN

TECHNICAL EDITOR: BARBARA SMITH

BOOK DESIGN/ILLUSTRATIONS: ANGELA SCHADE & LISA M. CLARK

COVER DESIGN: MICHAEL BUCKINGHAM

PHOTOGRAPHY: CHARLES R. LYNCH

**Library of Congress Cataloging-in-Publication Data**

Purney-Mark, Susan.

      Quilted havens : city houses, country homes / Susan Purney-Mark & Daphne Greig.

                  p.            cm.

      ISBN 1-57432-731-3

      1. Quilting--Patterns.  2. Appliqué--Patterns   3. Embroidery--Patterns.

4. Dwellings in art.

quilts--United States--History.              I. Greig, Daphne.     II. Title.

TT835.P87             1999

746.46--dc21                             99-059946

                                                 CIP

Additional copies of this book may be ordered from the American Quilter's Society, PO Box 3290, Paducah, KY 42002-3290 @ $22.95. Add $2.00 for postage and handling.

We have had a great amount of fun in creating this book for you to use and enjoy. Nothing is created without the help from others and we gratefully dedicate *Quilted Havens – City Houses, Country Homes* to those who have helped us in so many ways.

First, to our friends who tested our designs and read the directions we thank: Amy Andreasen, Jean Avison, Rose Bates, Janet Beitz, Wendy Birch, Kathy Black, Sheila Cahill, Aileen Conway, Anne Dalgliesh, Darlene Dressler, Peggy Estey, Jill Gardener, Joan Gorrill, Denise Gunn, Cindy Hultsch, Julie Jackson, Joanne Manzer, Avis Michalovsky, Barbara Murphy, Joyce Newman, Dot Stutter, Moira Sullivan, Patti Thomas, and Debbie Whitfield.

Second, to Robyn Whitbread and the staff at Satin Moon Quilt Shop, Victoria, British Columbia, your encouragement and support have been invaluable.

We thank the staff at American Quilter's Society for their expertise and guidance in seeing this book through to completion; in particular we thank Mary Jo Kurten, Barbara Smith, Shelley Hawkins, Angela Schade, and Lisa Clark.

And most importantly, to our families, Alan, Lindsay and Scott; Henry, Bronwen, Jocelyn, Arland and Allyson, you have given us the love and firm pushes we needed to see our book through to completion. Many thanks for the meals, taxi service, and clean loads of laundry.

**ACKNOWLEDGMENTS**

**CONTENTS**

Introduction . . . . . . . . . . . . . . . . . . . . . . . . . . . . . . . . . . . . . . . . . . .5

House and Home Projects . . . . . . . . . . . . . . . . . . . . . . . . . . . . . . . .6

    School Days . . . . . . . . . . . . . . . . . . . . . . . . . . . . . . . . . .7

    Our Home and Native Land . . . . . . . . . . . . . . . . . . . . . .15

    A Sampling of Houses . . . . . . . . . . . . . . . . . . . . . . . . . .22

    Gingerbread House . . . . . . . . . . . . . . . . . . . . . . . . . . . .30

    The House Around the Corner . . . . . . . . . . . . . . . . . . . .36

    Victorian Manor . . . . . . . . . . . . . . . . . . . . . . . . . . . . . .42

    Thimbleville . . . . . . . . . . . . . . . . . . . . . . . . . . . . . . . . .46

    Gnome Homes . . . . . . . . . . . . . . . . . . . . . . . . . . . . . . .50

    Log Cabin Retreat . . . . . . . . . . . . . . . . . . . . . . . . . . . .57

    Hillbilly Hotel . . . . . . . . . . . . . . . . . . . . . . . . . . . . . . . .65

Group Project . . . . . . . . . . . . . . . . . . . . . . . . . . . . . . . . . . . . . . .69

    Donation Dwelling . . . . . . . . . . . . . . . . . . . . . . . . . . . .70

Piece by Piece, Build Your Home . . . . . . . . . . . . . . . . . . . . . . . . .74

General Quiltmaking Techniques . . . . . . . . . . . . . . . . . . . . . . . . .84

It is our hope that every reader will find something appealing in this book and that each one will have an opportunity to learn something new, whether it is a technique, a design, or a different approach to a familiar topic. *Quilted Havens* is also meant to encourage the quilter to personalize the information, using the ideas as a jumping-off point for exploration. The projects offer a variety of techniques, sizes, and skill levels, and we have designed the projects so that people of all ages can enjoy working together on them.

*Quilted Havens* explores a topic of significance to all quilters. Each of us has a home, and the love of home and hearth ties us closely together. It is a universal need for us to have shelter to keep us warm and safe and to have a sanctuary where the outside world can be kept at bay for at least a short span of time.

Our homes have a great deal to say about who we are, how we live, and our values as individuals, as families, and as a society. The welcoming home of a friend or relative can envelop us like a warm blanket, nurturing our bodies as well as our souls. So come visit our "homes," enjoy what we offer, invite your friends over, and we can all learn from one another.

"Donation Dwelling" is a special pattern we designed to be made by charity groups or quilt guilds for fund raising or donations. This pattern can be copied as needed for fund raising purposes. The chapter is written as a three-act play, and quilters can take on the roles of the characters and have some fun! This quilt is suitable for a raffle or for display on a wall or bed in a shelter or transition house. As quilters, we are blessed with skills that can help provide warmth and comfort, and we believe we are obliged to share these skills for the benefit of others. So, please, get a group together and make a quilt to warm someone's body and soul.

"Piece by Piece, Build Your Home" offers information on expanding the projects by using other techniques, such as photo transfer, embellishment, and fabric manipulation. We especially hope our book encourages you to think about your own home and how you might portray it in fabric.

Have fun, be confident, and we are certain that many havens will be built with joy.

# House &

# Home

Quilted Havens – Susan Purney-Mark and Daphne Greig

# School Days

*I have had playmates,*
*I have had companions,*
*In my days of childhood,*
*in my joyful school days.*

*Charles Lamb*

This wallhanging could be a wonderful gift for a favorite teacher or a great beginner's project. This quilt offers an easy way to learn to use templates and combine them with rotary cutting. We have used a lively children's novelty print, which is a one-way print, so be careful when planning your cutting. You could replace the letters and numbers with names or dates to commemorate a special event.

*SCHOOL DAYS by Susan Purney-Mark*
*Finished size: 32" x 32"*

## Supplies
### for a 32" x 32" quilt

| Fabrics | Yardage |
| --- | --- |
| Main (inner triangles, borders, and binding) | 1⅛ |
| Light (background) | ½ |
| Four medium prints (schoolhouse) | fat quarter each |
| Backing | 1 (36" x 36") |
| Batting | 36" x 36" |

# CUTTING

## Schoolhouse

From the Schoolhouse patterns starting on page 10, trace patches on template plastic or lightweight cardboard. Do not add seam allowances to the templates. Cut out the templates and trace them on the wrong side of the fabrics. Add ¼" seam allowances by eye as you cut out the fabric patches. With this method, you will have an accurate marked line for sewing by hand or machine.

## Inner Triangles

From the main fabric, cut two squares 9⅜". Cut each in half diagonally for four triangles.

## Outer Triangles

From light background fabric, cut two squares 12⅞". Cut each in half diagonally for four triangles.

## Borders

From light background fabric, cut four strips 4½" x 24½".

## Corner Squares

Cut four squares 4½", one from each medium print.

# SEWING

To sew the patches together, match seam lines by inserting a pin through the marked seams of both patches (Fig. 1).

Fig. 1. Insert pin through marked seam lines of both patches for accurate stitching.

1. Arrange the schoolhouse pieces to match the assembly diagram on page 14.

After sewing each piece, return the unit to the layout to help keep your pieces in order.

2. Join all window units (pieces A and J).

3. Add three H pieces to the longer window unit. Then add piece G to form a square.

4. Add pieces F and K to the other window unit.

5. Join roof pieces E and D.

6. Join the two house units to the roof unit. Where the three seams meet, stop stitching ¼" from the edge to help the pieces lie flat.

7. Join the A, B, C, and Cr (reverse) pieces to form a crescent-shaped unit. (Hint: Stop stitching ¼" away from the bottom edge of pieces C and Cr.) Add this unit to the house unit to complete the block. Press. Measure the block and trim to 12½".

## QUILT ASSEMBLY

### Sewing Quilt Top

1. To join triangles (cut from the main fabric) to the schoolhouse block, sew two triangles to opposite sides of the block, then sew two triangles to the remaining sides. The resulting square should measure 17½". Trim, if necessary.

2. Repeat Step 1 with the triangles cut from the background fabric. The square should measure 24½". Trim, if necessary.

3. Add one border strip to each of the two vertical sides of the quilt.

4. Join one corner block to each end of the two remaining border strips, then add these units to the top and bottom of the quilt.

### Appliqué

Make template for letters, numbers, or your own desired subject matter. Use templates to cut pieces and appliqué in place. Remember to trace templates in reverse so appliqué will be in proper order.

Refer to General Quiltmaking Techniques (page 88), for appliqué directions.

### Finishing

Mark the quilting design of your choice on the top. In this project, words that school children might use are quilted. Perhaps you could personalize it with a teacher's name and important dates.

Layer the backing, batting, and quilt top. Quilt as marked. Make and apply binding as shown in General Quiltmaking Techniques (page 94). Add a hanging sleeve and label.

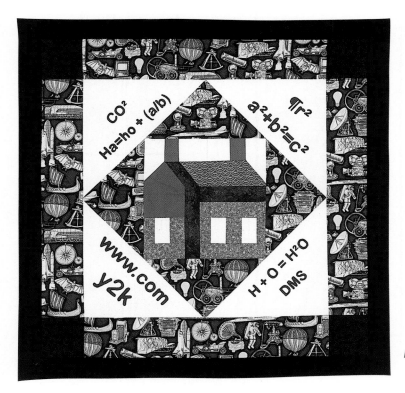

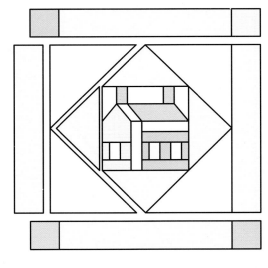

*Quilt layout*

*MILLENNIUM by Avis Michalovsky*

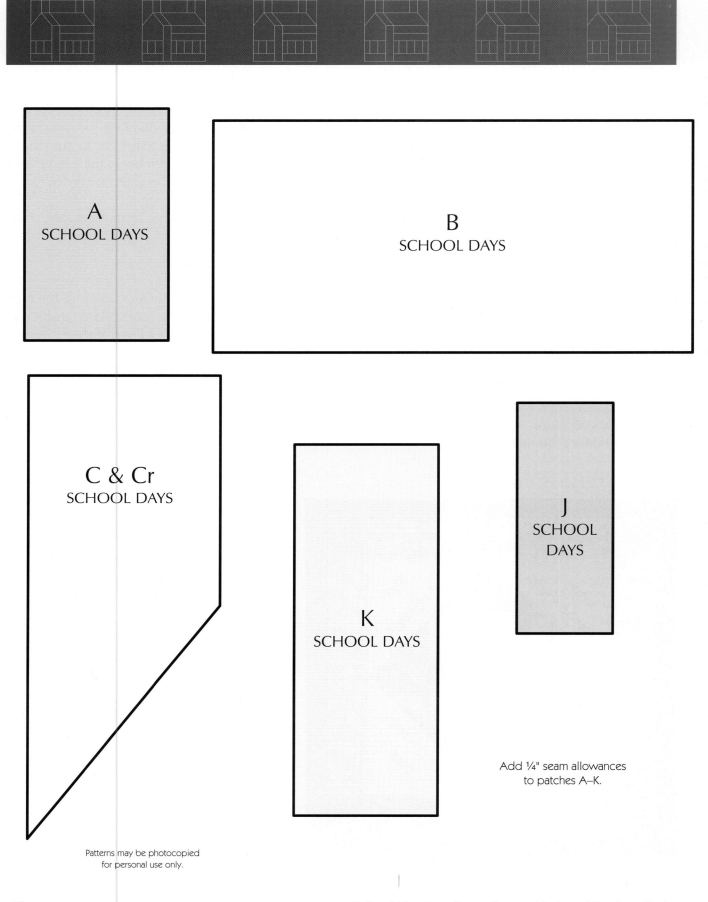

A
SCHOOL DAYS

B
SCHOOL DAYS

C & Cr
SCHOOL DAYS

J
SCHOOL
DAYS

K
SCHOOL DAYS

Add ¼" seam allowances
to patches A–K.

Patterns may be photocopied
for personal use only.

Quilted Havens – Susan Purney-Mark and Daphne Greig

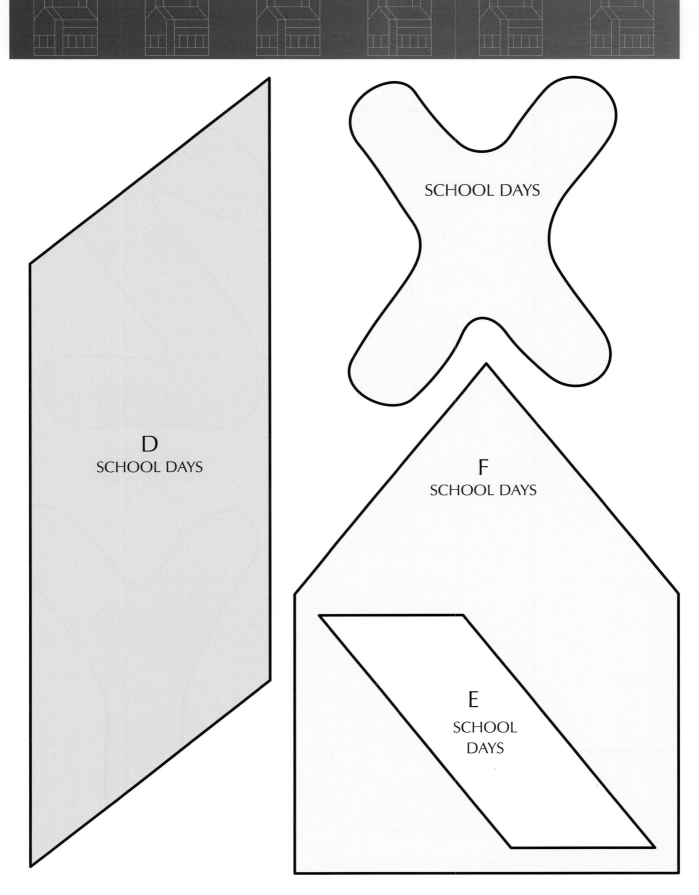

D
SCHOOL DAYS

SCHOOL DAYS

F
SCHOOL DAYS

E
SCHOOL
DAYS

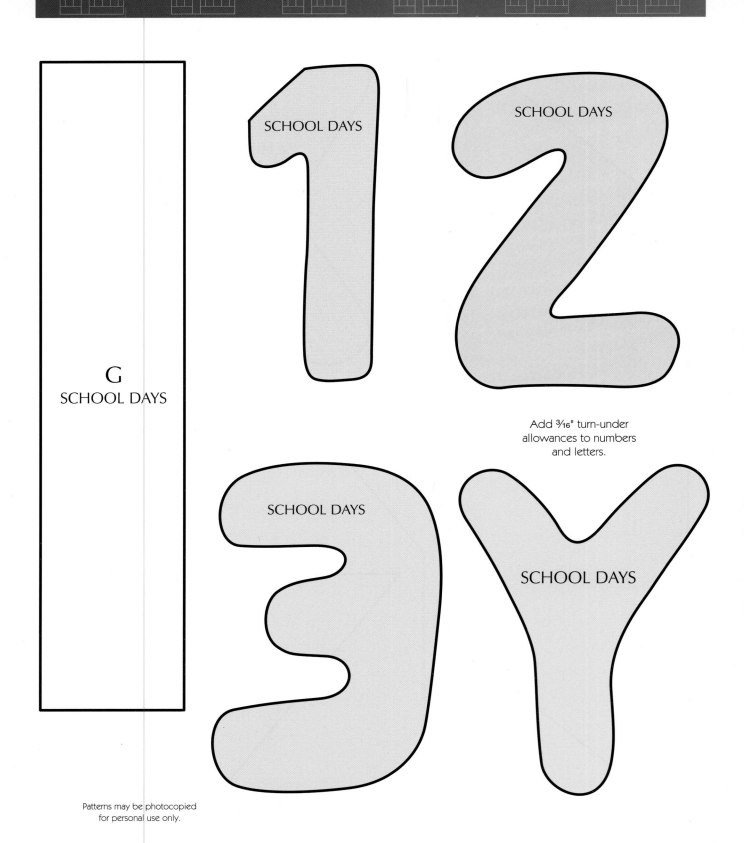

G
SCHOOL DAYS

SCHOOL DAYS

SCHOOL DAYS

Add ³⁄₁₆" turn-under allowances to numbers and letters.

SCHOOL DAYS

SCHOOL DAYS

Patterns may be photocopied
for personal use only.

Quilted Havens – Susan Purney-Mark and Daphne Greig

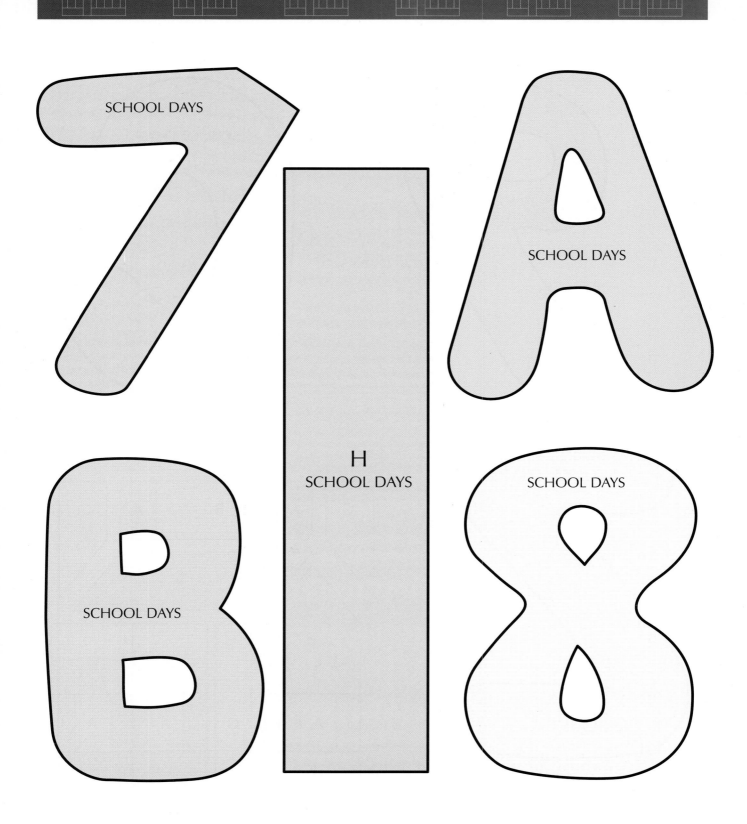

SCHOOL DAYS

SCHOOL DAYS

H
SCHOOL DAYS

SCHOOL DAYS

SCHOOL DAYS

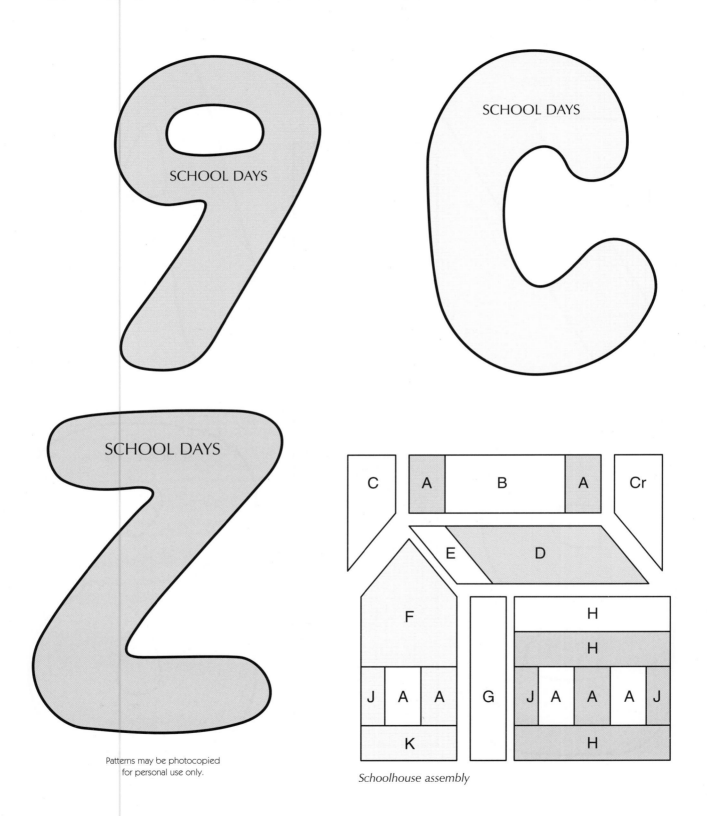

SCHOOL DAYS

SCHOOL DAYS

SCHOOL DAYS

Patterns may be photocopied
for personal use only.

*Schoolhouse assembly*

**Quilted Havens – Susan Purney-Mark and Daphne Greig**

# Our Home and Native Land

*It's the great, big, broad land 'way up yonder,*
*It's the forests where silence has lease;*
*It's the beauty that thrills me with wonder,*
*It's the stillness that fills me with peace.*

Robert W. Service, "The Spell of the Yukon"

Houses are not always made of wood or brick. In Canada's Far North, the traditional winter dwelling was an igloo made of blocks of ice and snow. We are proud of our Canadian heritage and invite you to create a remembrance of our northern lands.

*OUR HOME AND NATIVE LAND by Daphne Greig*
*Finished size: 34" x 34"*

## Supplies
### for a 34" x 34" quilt

| Fabrics | Yardage |
|---|---|
| Northern lights (sky) | ¾ |
| Snow | ½ |
| Ground under igloos | ¼ |
| Igloos | ⅛ |
| Polar bears | ⅛ |
| Ground under polar bears | ⅛ |
| Fishers:<br>   jackets, fur, pants,<br>   boots, pond, ice,<br>   and spearhead | scraps |
| Border | ¾ |
| Thin batting:<br>   place under igloos and<br>   bears to prevent<br>   shadowing | ¼ |
| Binding | ⅜ |
| Backing | 1⅛ (38" x 38") |
| Batting | 38" x 38" |

Machine embroidery threads for satin-stitch

Fusible web

## CUTTING

### Northern Lights

Five 4½" x 8½" rectangles for igloo panel
One 8½" x 20½" rectangle
Two strips, 2" x width of fabric for polar bear panel

### Snow

One 14½" x 20½" rectangle
Two strips 2" x 21" for three-dimensional horizon line

### Ground under Igloos

Five 2½" x 8½" rectangles

### Ground under Bears

One 1½" x 20½" strip

### Border

Four strips, 2" x width of fabric for polar bear panel
Six strips, 2½" x width of fabric

## SEWING

### Igloo Panel

Sew the 4½" x 8½" northern lights rectangles and ground rectangles together alternately to make the background units for the igloos, beginning with northern lights at the top. The sewn panel should measure 8½" x 30½".

### Fisher Panel

1. Place the two 2" strips of snow fabric right sides together. Draw a random shallow curve along one long edge (Fig. 2). Sew along this line, using a short machine stitch (approximately 18 stitches per inch). Trim the seam allowance to ⅛" and turn right side out. Press. Trim to an average width of 1". This piece will form a three-dimensional horizon edge.

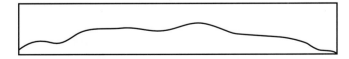

Fig. 2. Draw a random shallow curve on snow fabric.

2. Place the 8½" x 20½" northern lights rectangle and the 14½" x 20½" snow rectangle right sides together

Quilted Havens – Susan Purney-Mark and Daphne Greig

with the raw horizon edge in between. Match all the raw edges and sew with a ¼" seam allowance. Press the allowance toward the snow so the horizon edge covers the straight seam as shown in Fig. 3.

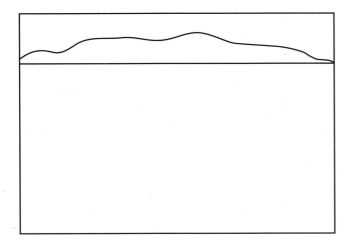

*Fig. 3. Sew three-dimensional horizon edge in the seam.*

## Polar Bear Panel

1. A Seminole-piecing technique is used to create the northern lights effect behind the polar bears. Cut the two 2" strips of northern lights fabric in half to make four pieces 2" x approximately 22". Cut the four 2" strips of border fabric in half to make eight pieces 2" x approximately 22". Sew strips in two sets as shown in Fig. 4.

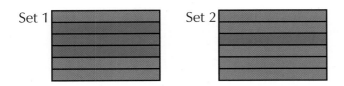

*Fig. 4. Sew two sets of strips. The blue strips represent the northern lights.*

2. Press the seam allowances of Set 1 down and the allowances of Set 2 up. Cut ten 2" segments from each set, keeping the segments of each set separate.

3. Lay out the segments alternately, as shown in Fig.

5, offsetting the top of the strips as shown. Sew the segments together with a ¼" seam allowance and match the seams for each square. Press the seam allowances of the pieced strip in one direction.

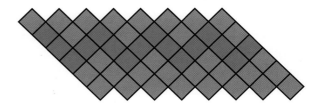

*Fig. 5. Offset strips to make northern lights.*

4. Select and cut your favorite 20½" of the strip and trim as follows: Carefully align a ruler along the top edge and trim, leaving a ¼" seam allowance beyond the points. Measure 5½" from the trimmed edge and trim the lower edge. Sew the 1½" x 20½" strip of ground to this lower edge. The unit should now measure 6½" x 20½". To stabilize the top edge before appliquéing the polar bears, sew one of the 2½" border strips to the top.

## APPLIQUÉ

1. Trace the appliqué images on the paper backing of the fusible web. (The patterns are reversed so they will appear as in the quilt when fused to your fabrics.) Cut apart, leaving space around each image.

2. Following manufacturer's directions, fuse the traced images to the wrong side of selected fabrics. When cool, cut out each piece with sharp scissors. Remove the paper backing.

3. Use the paper backing from the igloo and the polar bear as a pattern to cut the same shapes from thin batting. Cut five igloos and three polar bears from the batting. Trim ¼" from all edges and position the batting under the appliqués as you arrange them on the background. The batting will prevent the panel fabrics from shadowing through the igloos and polar bears.

4. Arrange all the pieces on the panels by using the photograph and dashed markings on the patterns as guides. When you are happy with the placement, fuse the pieces on the panels, following the manufacturer's directions.

5. Using a fine satin stitch and matching machine embroidery thread, stitch around each piece. Use tan or gray thread to stitch the lines on the igloo. See General Quiltmaking Techniques for machine satin stitch instructions (page 90).

## QUILT ASSEMBLY

Refer to the quilt panel layout. Sew the polar bear panel to the fisher panel. Sew 2½" border strips between this unit and the igloo panel and to the sides of the quilt. Sew 2½" border strips to the top and bottom of the quilt. Press the quilt carefully.

### *Stamping*

As an added embellishment for this project, stamp snowflakes along the borders near the top of the quilt. See Piece by Piece (page 81) for information on using this technique.

### *Finishing*

Layer the quilt with batting and backing and baste well. Quilt around the appliqués and quilt accent lines in the sky (northern lights) and in the snow. Make and apply binding as shown in General Quiltmaking Techniques (page 94). Add a hanging sleeve and label.

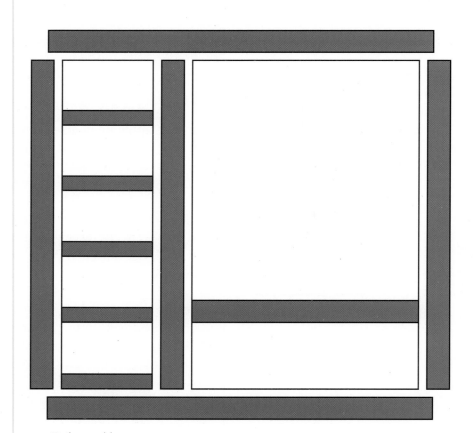

*Quilt panel layout*

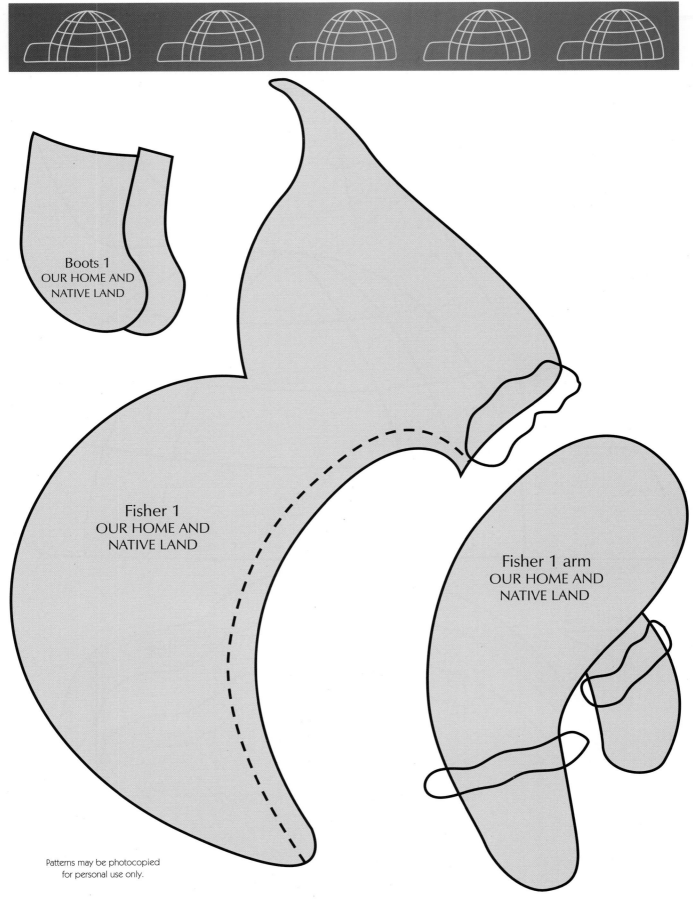

Boots 1
OUR HOME AND
NATIVE LAND

Fisher 1
OUR HOME AND
NATIVE LAND

Fisher 1 arm
OUR HOME AND
NATIVE LAND

Patterns may be photocopied
for personal use only.

**Quilted Havens – Susan Purney-Mark and Daphne Greig**

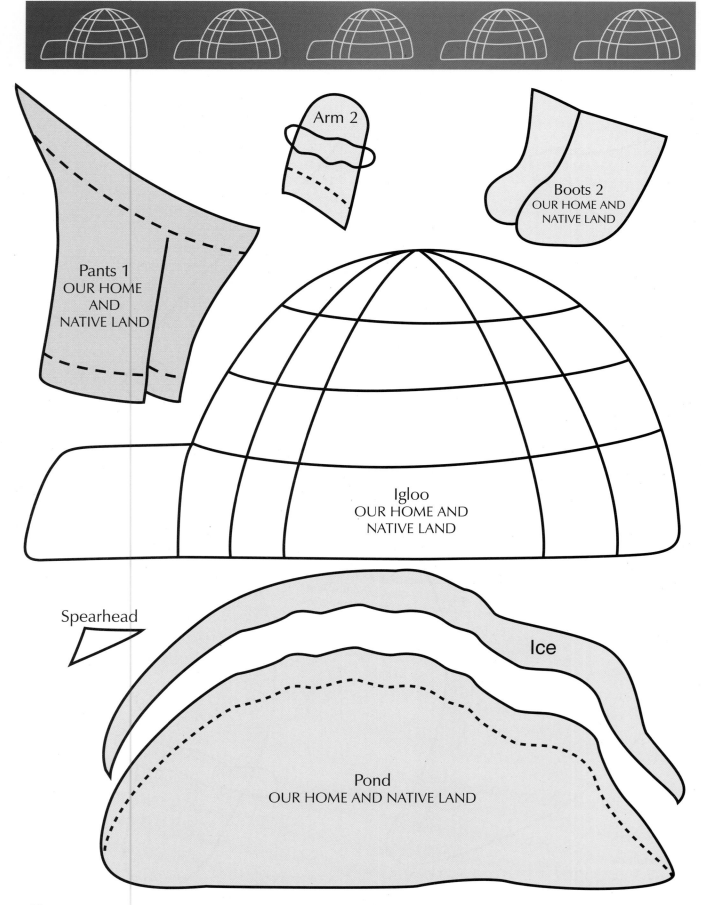

Arm 2

Boots 2
OUR HOME AND
NATIVE LAND

Pants 1
OUR HOME
AND
NATIVE LAND

Igloo
OUR HOME AND
NATIVE LAND

Spearhead

Ice

Pond
OUR HOME AND NATIVE LAND

Quilted Havens – Susan Purney-Mark and Daphne Greig

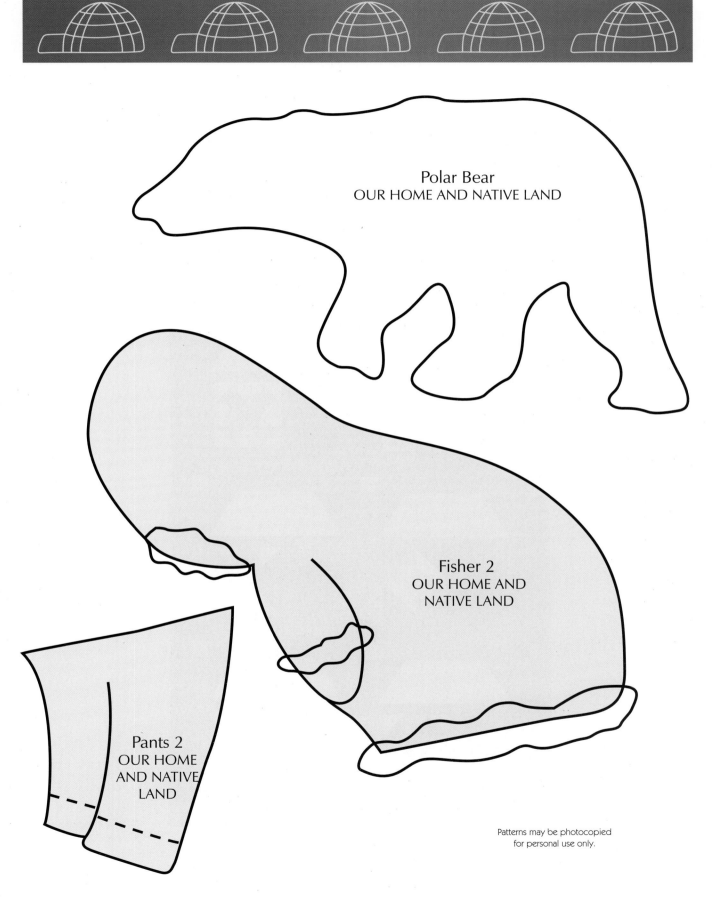

Polar Bear
OUR HOME AND NATIVE LAND

Fisher 2
OUR HOME AND
NATIVE LAND

Pants 2
OUR HOME
AND NATIVE
LAND

Patterns may be photocopied
for personal use only.

# A Sampling of Houses

*But every house where Love abides*
*And Friendship is a guest,*
*Is surely home, and home sweet home;*
*For there the heart can rest.*

*Henry Van Dyke, "Home Song"*

This fun quilt combines two popular themes, house blocks and sampler blocks, and it is suitable for confident beginners. First, cut and construct the six sampler blocks. Then select fabrics for the six houses that will complement and coordinate with the sampler blocks.

*A SAMPLING OF HOUSES by Patti Thomas*
*Finished size: 33" x 48"*

Quilted Havens – Susan Purney-Mark and Daphne Greig

## Supplies
### for a 33" x 48" quilt

| Fabrics | Yardage |
|---|---|
| Houses | Variety of scraps (at least 12) totaling approx. 2 yds. Six pieces (at least 6" x 12") for roofs. |
| Sashing | ¾ |
| Backing | 1⅝ (37" x 52") |
| Batting | 37" x 52" |
| Binding | ¾ |

## SAMPLER BLOCKS

Use a wide variety of fabrics for the six sampler blocks. Cutting instructions for each block identify the fabrics by value: light, medium, and dark. For best results, use fabrics of the values listed for each of the block sections. Each sampler block should measure 6½" unfinished.

Several of the sampler blocks have half-square triangle units. For our favorite method of making these units, we use squares cut from two contrasting fabrics. The individual block instructions will tell you what size squares to use, but here is the basic method:

1. First, mark a diagonal line, corner to corner, on the wrong side of the lighter square. Draw two lines ¼" away from this line.

2. Layer this square with a darker square, right sides together, and sew on the outer two lines. Cut along the center diagonal line and press the seam allowances toward the darker fabric. Trim the squares to the measurement given in the individual block instructions.

(Be sure that the diagonal seam line runs exactly corner to corner after trimming.) Each pair of squares will make two half-square triangle units.

# Block 1 – Farm Friendliness

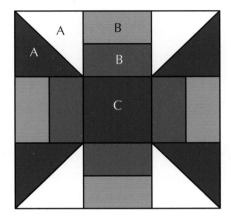

## Cutting

| Light | Two | 2⅞" squares (A) |
|---|---|---|
| Medium-1 | Four | 1½" x 2½" rectangles (B) |
| Medium-2 | Four | 1½" x 2½" rectangles (B) |
| Dark | Two | 2⅞" squares (A) |
| | One | 2½" square (C) |

## Sewing

1. Make four half-square triangle units; using two light and two dark A squares. Trim units to measure 2½".

2. Sew the medium-1 and medium-2 rectangles together in pairs along the long edge. Press seam allowances toward the medium-2 fabric.

3. Arrange and sew the block units together in rows. Then sew the rows together.

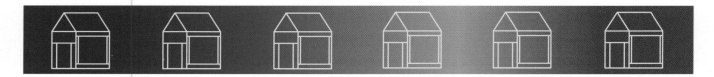

## Block 2 – Aunt Vina Variation

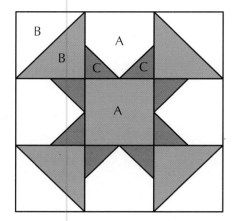

### Cutting

| | | |
|---|---|---|
| Light-1 | Four | 2½" squares (A) |
| Light-2 | Two | 2⅞" squares (B) |
| Medium | One | 2½" square (A) |
| | Two | 2⅞" squares (B) |
| Dark | Eight | 1½" squares (C) |

### Sewing

1. Make four half-square triangle units from the light-2 and medium B squares. Trim units to measure 2½".

2. Mark a diagonal line, corner to corner, on the wrong side of each dark C square. Place a C square in the corner of a light-1 A square, right sides together, sew diagonally; trim.

3. Repeat on the other corner to make the corner-square unit. Make a total of four units.

4. Arrange and sew block units together in rows. Then sew the rows together.

## Block 3 – Prairie Queen

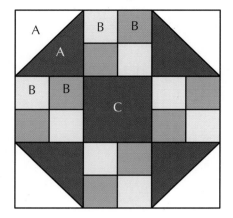

### Cutting

| | | |
|---|---|---|
| Light | Two | 2⅞" squares (A) |
| Medium-1 | Eight | 1½" squares (B) |
| Medium-2 | Eight | 1½" squares (B) |
| Dark | Two | 2⅞" squares (A) |
| | One | 2½" square (C) |

### Sewing

1. Make four half-square triangle units using two light and two dark A squares. Trim units to measure 2½".

2. Sew the medium-1 and medium-2 B squares together in pairs. Press seam allowances toward medium-2. Sew two of these units together to form a four-patch unit.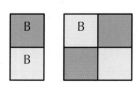

3. Arrange and sew the block units together in rows. Then sew the rows together.

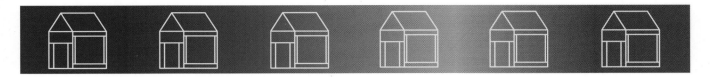

## Block 4 – Next Door Neighbor

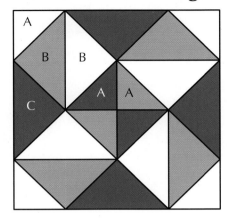

### Cutting

| Light | Two | 2⅜" squares cut in half diagonally (A) |
| | Two | 3" squares cut in half diagonally (B) |
| Medium | One | 2⅜" square cut in half diagonally (A) |
| | Two | 3" squares cut in half diagonally (B) |
| Dark | One | 2⅜" square cut in half diagonally (A) |
| | One | 4¼" square cut in half twice diagonally (C) |

### Sewing

1. Sew the medium and dark A triangles together to form the center quarter-square unit.

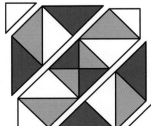

2. Sew the medium and light B triangles together to form four half-square units.

3. Sew the units, side and corner triangles.

## Block 5 – Kaleidoscope

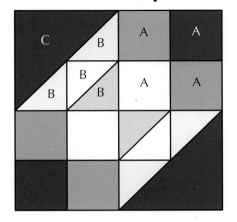

### Cutting

| Light–1 | Two | 2" squares (A) |
| | One | 2⅜" square cut in half diagonally (B) |
| Light–2 | Two | 2⅜" squares cut in half diagonally (B) |
| Medium | One | 2⅜" square cut in half diagonally (B) |
| Medium–Dark | Four | 2" squares (A) |
| Dark | Two | 2" squares (A) |
| | One | 3⅞" square cut in half diagonally (C) |

### Sewing

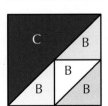

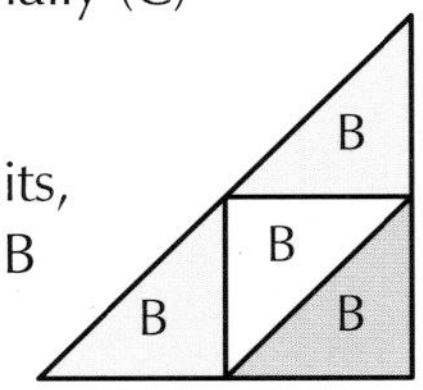

1. Make two half-square triangle units, using one light–1 and one medium B triangle. Trim to 2".

2. Sew two light–2 triangles (B) to each of the half-square triangles.

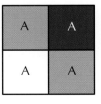

3. Sew a dark triangle (C) to each of these units.

4. Make two four-patch blocks from light–1, medium–dark, and dark A squares.

5. Arrange the four units and sew them together to form the block.

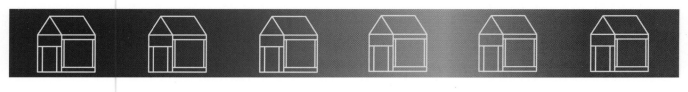

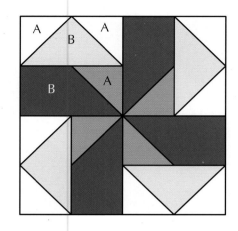

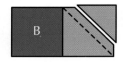  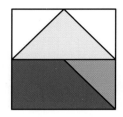

## Block 6 – Seesaw
### Cutting

| Light | Eight | 2" squares (A) |
|---|---|---|
| Medium-1 | Four | 2" x 3½" rectangles (B) |
| Medium-2 | Four | 2" x 3½" rectangles (B) |
| Dark | Four | 2" squares (A) |

### Sewing

1. Place a light A square on a medium-1 B rectangle and sew diagonally through the square, corner to corner. Trim the excess triangles, leaving a ¼" seam

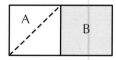

allowance. Press the triangle open.

2. Repeat on the other half of the rectangle with another light square to make the finished unit. Make three more of these units.

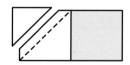

3. Place a dark A square on a medium-2 B rectangle and sew diagonally through the dark square, corner to corner. Trim the excess triangles, leaving a ¼" seam allowance. Press the triangle open.

4. Sew the units together in pairs.

5. Arrange the four units and sew them together to form the block.

## GENERAL HOUSE CONSTRUCTION

### Roof Section

Using templates A, B, C, and Cr (page 28–29), trace and cut pieces from fabric scraps. Sew the pieces together, as shown in Fig. 6. The roof section should measure 4½" x 12½" unfinished.

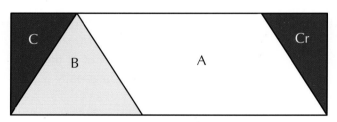

Fig. 6. Roof section

### Door Section

| House Fabric | One | 3" x 5½" rectangle (F) |
|---|---|---|
| | Two | 1½" x 6" rectangles (E) |
| Door Fabric | One | 3½" x 6" rectangle (D) |

Sew one E rectangle to each side of the D rectangle. Press seam allowances away from door. Sew rectangle F to the top of this unit. Press allowances away from door (Fig. 7). The door section should measure 5½" x 8½".

Quilted Havens – Susan Purney-Mark and Daphne Greig

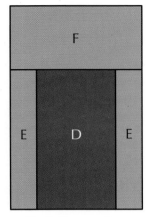

Fig. 7. Door section

## Block Section

| House Fabric | Two | 1" x 6½" strips (G) |
|---|---|---|
| | Two | 1½" x 7½" strips (H) |

Add G strips to two opposite sides of each sampler block previously constructed. Sew the H strips to the remaining sides (Fig. 8). Press seam allowances toward the house fabric. The block sections should measure 7½" x 8½".

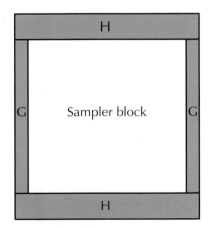

Fig. 8. Side of house

## Put the House Together

Sew the sampler block section to the door section and then sew this combined unit to the roof section (Fig. 9). The finished block should measure 12½".

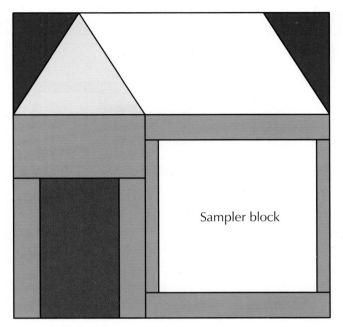

Fig. 9. Completed house

## QUILT ASSEMBLY

### Sashing and Cornerstones

1. Cut six strips across the sashing fabric (selvage to selvage) each 3½" wide. Cut these strips into 17 segments, each 12½" long.

2. Make 12 four-patch blocks for the cornerstones from a variety of 2" squares cut from the house fabrics.

3. Arrange the sashing strips and the four-patch blocks with the house blocks (see Quilt layout, page 28). Sew together in rows and then sew the rows together. Press all the seam allowances toward the sashing strips.

### Finishing

Layer the quilt with batting and backing and baste well. Quilt where desired. Try adding texture to the roofs by quilting scallops. Quilt rectangles in the doors to resemble wood-paneled doors. Make and apply binding as shown in General Quiltmaking Techniques (page 94). Add a hanging sleeve and label.

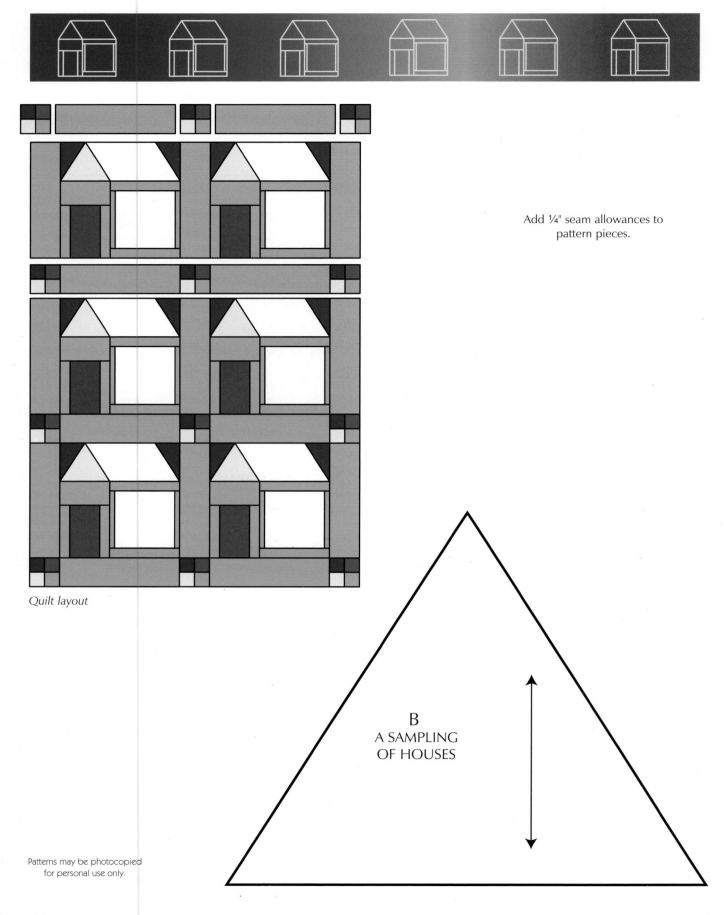

Add ¼" seam allowances to pattern pieces.

*Quilt layout*

B
A SAMPLING
OF HOUSES

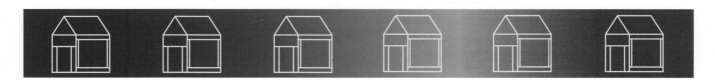

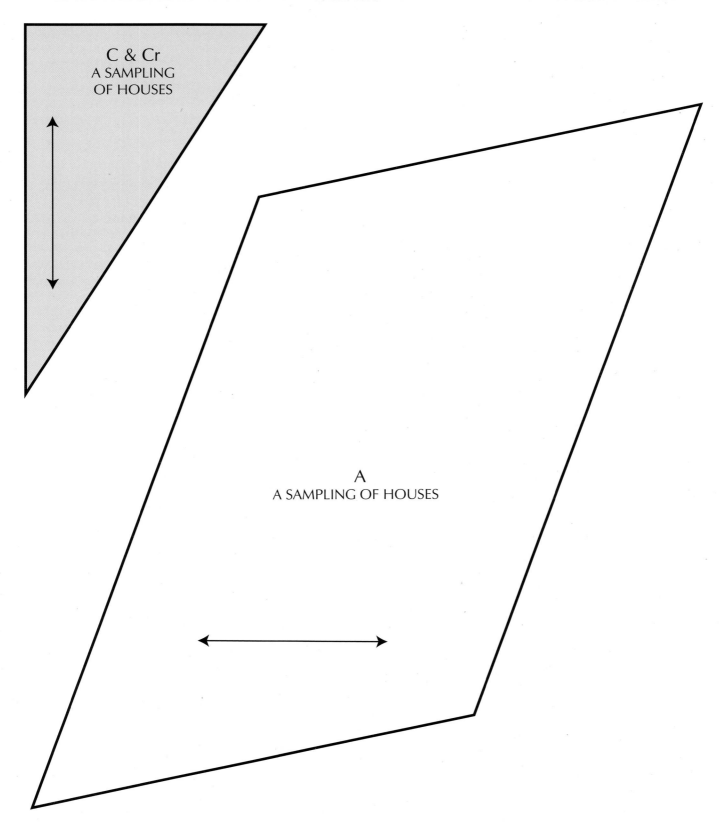

C & Cr
A SAMPLING
OF HOUSES

A
A SAMPLING OF HOUSES

# Gingerbread House

*And when they approached the little house*
*they saw that it was built of bread and covered with cakes,*
*but that the windows were of clear sugar.*

The Brothers Grimm, "Hansel and Gretel"

Popular buttonhole appliqué is featured in this project. Stitching can be done by hand or machine. See General Quilting Techniques (Appliqué, pages 88–91) for instructions. A variety of embellishments can be added. This wallhanging shown is made of felted wool for the background and rainbow felt for the appliqués. It is embellished with a variety of buttons.

*GINGERBREAD HOUSE by Daphne Greig*
*Finished size: 30" x 42"*

## Supplies
### for a 30" x 42" quilt

| Fabrics | Yardage |
| --- | --- |
| Background | 32" x 48" |
| House front | 13" x 18" |
| House side | 13" x 10" |
| Roof scallops | |
|    Light | 9" x 11" |
|    Dark | 12" x 11" |
| Roof edging | 4" x 13" |
| Window | 5" x 4" |
| Door | 6" x 9" |
| Pine tree | 10" x 14" |
| Tree trunk | 4" x 11" |
| Shrubs (2) | One 3" x 7" and One 3" x 6" |
| Stepping stones (7) | scraps |
| Layered flowers | Five 4" blue squares Three 3" red squares Two 3" cream squares |
| Buttons | 70 to 80 of various sizes |

*Gingerbread House Jacket by Jill Gardener*

Fabric amounts are for felt. Purchase twice the amount of fabric listed for the roof scallops, roof edging, and layered flowers if you plan to make the quilt from cotton fabrics.

This quilt can also be made in cotton fabrics, for example, plaids for a country theme, or Christmas prints to duplicate the look of traditional holiday gingerbread houses. See the instructions in Piece by Piece, page 78, for making three-dimensional appliqué for the roof scallops, edging, and flowers. We recommend using a fusible-web product to hold the other appliqués in place as you buttonhole stitch. Finish the wallhanging in the traditional manner (see General Quiltmaking Techniques, pages 93–95).

Another idea is to use the appliqués to embellish a jacket. Add two extra roof scallops when cutting. Our sample in the photo above shows gingerbread people running around the jacket. Trace these designs and add them near the bottom of the jacket.

## CUTTING

Cut all the appliqué pieces from the appropriate fabrics. (The appliqués are *not* reversed for the felt quilt. If you use a fusible-web product, trace the reversed images.) Use the scallop template to trace half circles around the bottom corners, sides, and bottom of the background fabric. Cut along the traced lines.

## APPLIQUÉS

1. Arrange the pieces on the background and sew in the following order: tree trunk, pine tree, house front, house side, window, and door.

2. For roof edging and scallops, sew along straight edge only, leaving sides and bottom unstitched. Overlap roof scallops approximately ¼".

3. Add shrubs and stepping stones.

4. Add your own special touches to the project. Fabric yo-yos with embroidered stems can form flowers. Ribbon embroidery will add a unique look. Check your button box for interesting buttons and beads.

## QUILT FINISHING

The quilt in the photo on page 30 is not layered with batting and backing. Felted wool is heavy and will hang nicely on its own, and the scalloped edge does not fray. Form a hanging pocket by turning the top 4" to the front. Buttonhole stitch in place. Layer a small flower on top of each large flower and secure them along the bottom of the hanging pocket by sewing a button in the center, through all the layers.

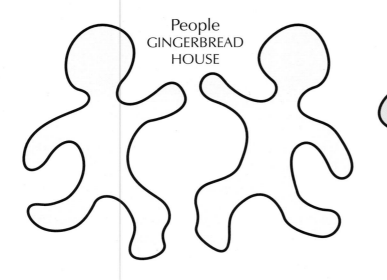

**People**
GINGERBREAD HOUSE

**Shrub**
GINGERBREAD HOUSE

Templates do not include turn-under allowances.

Enlarge pattern pieces 200% to make a 30" x 42" quilt, or use pattern "as is" for a smaller quilt or a garment.

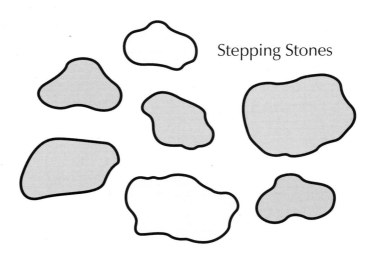

**Shrub**
GINGERBREAD HOUSE

**Stepping Stones**

**Quilted Havens – Susan Purney-Mark and Daphne Greig**

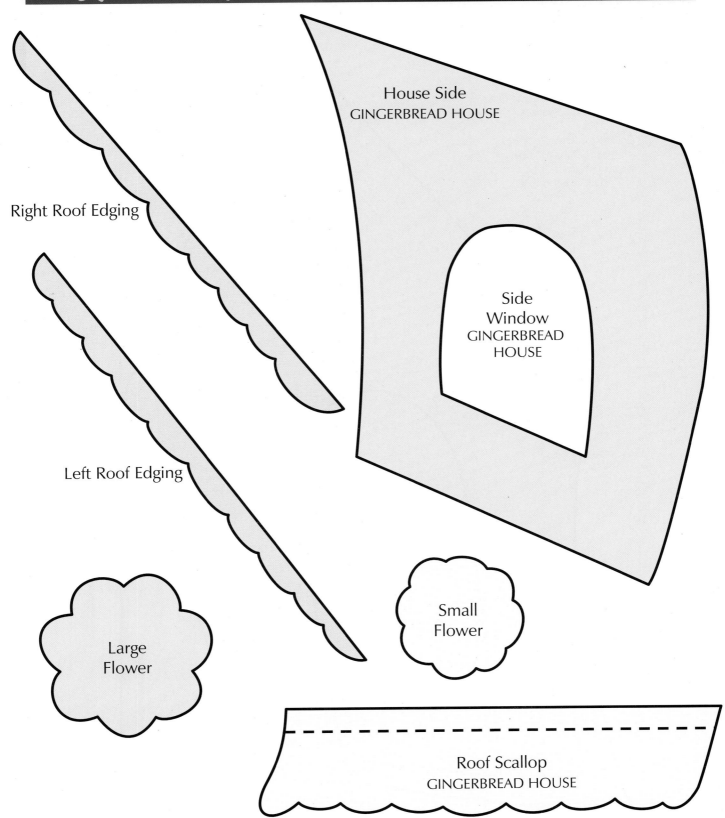

Right Roof Edging

Left Roof Edging

House Side
GINGERBREAD HOUSE

Side
Window
GINGERBREAD
HOUSE

Large
Flower

Small
Flower

Roof Scallop
GINGERBREAD HOUSE

Templates do not include turn-under allowances.

Enlarge pattern pieces 200% to make a 30" x 42" quilt, or use pattern "as is" for a smaller quilt or a garment.

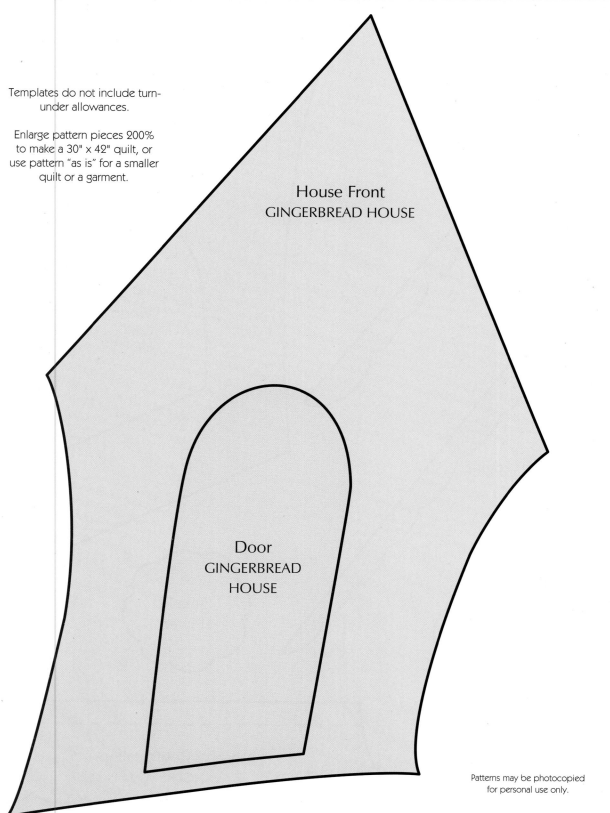

House Front
GINGERBREAD HOUSE

Door
GINGERBREAD
HOUSE

Patterns may be photocopied for personal use only.

Quilted Havens – Susan Purney-Mark and Daphne Greig

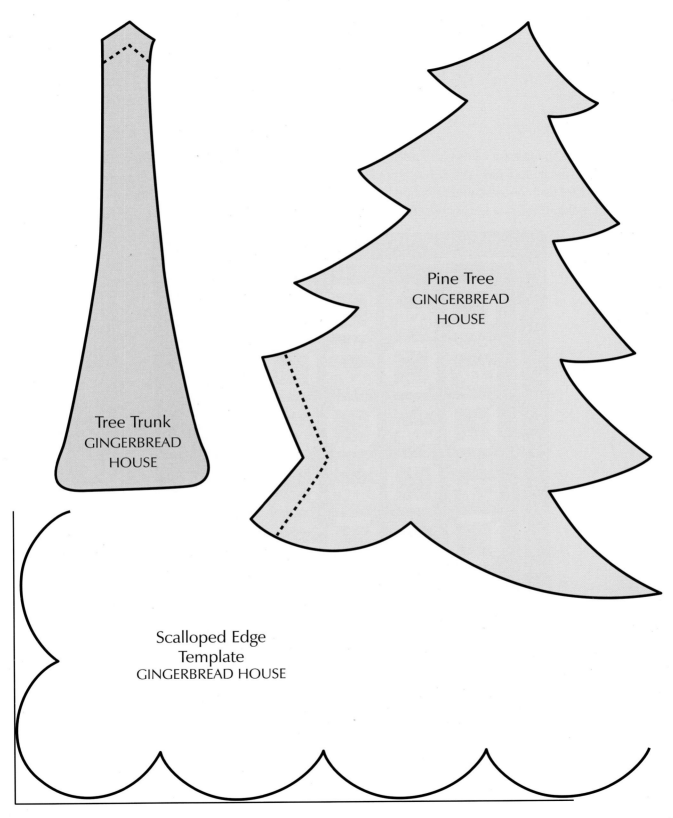

Pine Tree
GINGERBREAD
HOUSE

Tree Trunk
GINGERBREAD
HOUSE

Scalloped Edge
Template
GINGERBREAD HOUSE

# The House Around the Corner

*When the lamps of the house are lighted,*
*it is like the flowering*
*of the lotus upon the lake.*

*(Chinese Proverb)*

This quilt is suitable for all levels of ability, and it can be embellished with embroidery, buttons, or other special touches. We chose a floral print that simulates flowers and vines growing on the houses. Each house could be made from a different fabric to create a "neighborhood." You could make fewer blocks for a wallhanging or table runner.

*THE HOUSE AROUND THE CORNER by Janet Beitz, Moira Sullivan,*
*Patti Thomas, and Daphne Greig*
*Finished size: 69" x 88"*

## Supplies
### for a 69" x 88" quilt

| Fabrics | Yardage |
| --- | --- |
| Light-1<br>houses, border 2 | 1 |
| Light-2<br>chimneys, logs | 1 |
| Medium-1<br>windows, doors,<br>border 1, cornerstones<br>corner blocks | 2 |
| Medium-2<br>gables, grass, logs | 7/8 |
| Medium–3<br>Border 3, and binding | 2½ |
| Dark-1<br>sashing, roof,<br>four-patch | 1⅔ |
| Sky | ⅔ |
| Backing | 5 (73" x 92") |
| Batting | 73" x 92" |
| Paper for foundation<br>piecing | 2 |

## CUTTING

### House Blocks

Instructions are for one block. You can choose to work through each one to completion or do them in assembly-line fashion. Strips are cut across the width of the fabric, selvage to selvage. The patches for the foundation-pieced houses are cut oversized. After sewing, trim the blocks to size. Make 17 blocks 9½" square.

### Sky and Chimney Unit

| | |
| --- | --- |
| Sky | One 2" strip |
| Chimneys | Two 2" squares |

### Roof Unit

| | |
| --- | --- |
| Sky | Two 2½" x 3½" rectangles |
| Gable | One 4" square |
| Roof | One 4" x 9" rectangle |

### Door Unit

| | |
| --- | --- |
| House | One 2" strip |
| Door | One 2½" x 3½" rectangle |

### Window Unit

| | |
| --- | --- |
| Windows | One 2" strip |
| House | One 2" strip |

### Grass

| | |
| --- | --- |
| Grass | One 2" x 9½" rectangle |

### Cornerstone Blocks

Make 18 blocks 9½". Cut strips 2" wide across the width of the fabric, selvage to selvage. Cutting amounts are for all 18 blocks needed for the quilt.

| | |
| --- | --- |
| Light-2 | Twelve 2" strips |
| Medium-1 | Ten 2" strips. From strips cut 144 squares 2". Reserve two strips for the four-patch in the center. |
| Medium-2 | Six 2" strips |
| Dark-1 | Two 2" strips |

### Sashing

| | |
| --- | --- |
| Dark | Twenty-one 2" strips. Cut strips in 82 segments 2" x 9½". |
| Medium-1 | Four 2" strips. From strips cut 72 squares 2". |

## Border 1

Medium-1      Eight 2½" strips

## Border 2

Light-1      Eight 1½" strips

## Border 3

Medium-3      Four 5" strips. (You may want to cut this fabric lengthwise to eliminate joining seams.)

Medium-1      Four 5" squares for border

## SEWING

### House Blocks

Trace 17 houses (four units each) on foundation material. Refer to General Quiltmaking Techniques, page 91, for foundation-piecing instructions. Remember to sew the pieces for each unit in numerical order. Once the units are completed, join them in the following order:

1. Sew the sky/chimney unit to the roof unit.

2. Sew the door and window units together. (You can put the door unit on either side of the window unit.)

3. Join the sky/chimney and door/window units.

4. Add the 2" x 9½" rectangle of medium-2 to the lower edge for the grass.

5. Trim block to 9½". Repeat these steps to make the 17 blocks.

### Cornerstone Blocks

1. Join one medium-1 strip and one dark-1 strip

along their long sides. Repeat. Press and cut resulting strips into thirty-six 2" segments (Fig. 10).

2. Rotate and join two segments to form a four-patch unit (Fig. 11). Make 18 four-patch units.

3. Cut medium-2 strips into 72 rectangles 2" x 3½". Add one rectangle to each side of the four-patch unit (Fig. 12).

4. Join one medium-1 square (2" x 2") to each end of the 36 remaining medium-2 pieces. Add these units to the remaining sides of the block (Fig. 13).

5. Cut the light-2 strips into 72 rectangles 3" x 6½". Add the rectangles and squares as before to complete the 9½" block (Fig. 14). Make 18 blocks.

*Fig. 10. Cut sewn strips into 2" segments.*

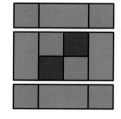

*Fig. 11. Join segments to make four-patch.*

*Fig. 12. Add a rectangle to each side.*

*Fig. 13. Add top and bottom pieces.*

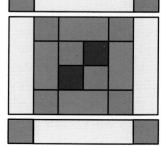

*Fig. 14. Add another "border" of squares and rectangles to complete block.*

## QUILT ASSEMBLY

1. For horizontal sashing, join five dark-1 strips into a unit with a medium-1 square between each strip and at each end. Make eight of these units (Fig. 15).

*Fig. 15. Horizontal sashing strips.*

2. Arrange the blocks in horizontal rows, alternating House and Cornerstone blocks. Place the vertical sashing strips between the blocks to separate them. Place the horizontal sashing units between each row. Join all units together.

3. For border 1, join two medium-1 strips, end to end, for each side of the quilt. Measure the length of the top and cut two borders that length from the joined strips. Sew strips to the sides of the quilt. Repeat for the top and bottom.

4. For border 2, join two light-1 border strips for each side of the quilt. Repeat measuring, cutting, and sewing as in Step 3.

5. For border 3, join strips as before unless borders were cut from lengthwise grain.

6. Measure the length of the quilt and cut two of the border-3 strips that length. Sew these borders to the sides of the quilt.

7. Measure and cut two strips for the top and bottom of the quilt.

8. Sew 5" medium-1 corner squares to each end of these strips and sew them to the quilt.

## FINISHING

Mark the quilting design on the top as desired. Layer backing, batting, and quilt top. Quilt as marked. Make and apply binding as shown in General Quilt-making Techniques (page 94). Add a hanging sleeve and label.

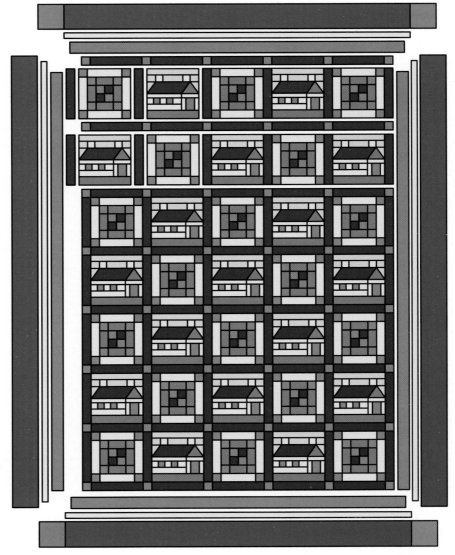

*Quilt layout*

When trimming, leave a ¼"
seam allowance around the outside of each unit.

| | |
|---|---|
| 4<br>House | 3<br>House |
| | Door unit<br>HOUSE AROUND<br>THE CORNER<br><br>1<br>Door |
| | 2<br>House |

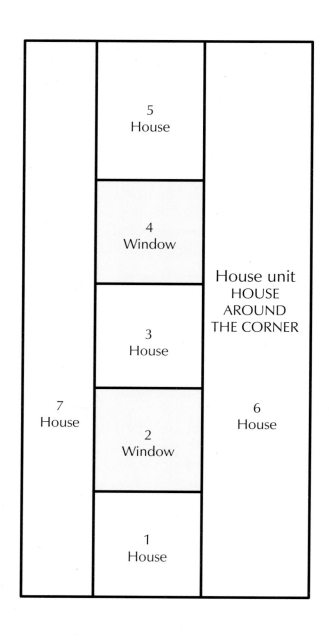

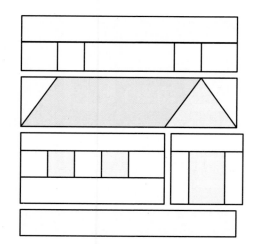

*Foundation piecing layout*

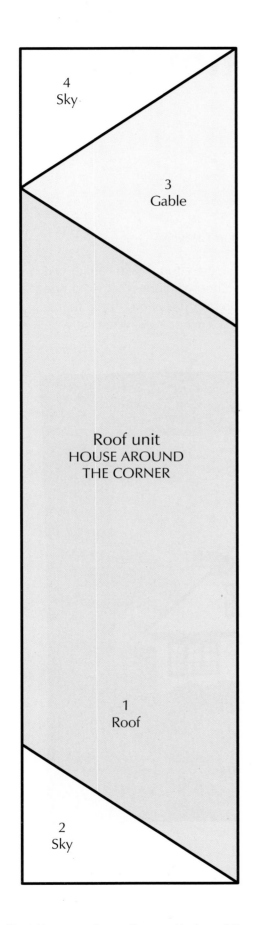

**4**
Sky

**3**
Gable

**Roof unit**
HOUSE AROUND
THE CORNER

**1**
Roof

**2**
Sky

**5**
Sky

**4**
Chimney

**Sky and**
**Chimney unit**

HOUSE
AROUND
THE CORNER

**3**
Sky

**2**
Chimney

**1**
Sky

**6**
Sky

# Victorian Manor

*Why do we love certain houses and*
*Why do they seem to love us?*
*It is the warmth of our individual hearts*
*Reflected in our surroundings.*
*T. H. Robsjon-Gibbings*

This is a challenging piece, but you will find it to be worth the extra effort. Make certain you understand the basics of foundation piecing. There are many "house" fabrics that would be lovely. You can try a white and brown combination, as pictured in the photo, for a Tudor-style mansion, or consider using stones and bricks for more of a frontier look. Whatever you choose, this wallhanging will claim center stage at home.

*VICTORIAN MANOR by Moira Sullivan*
*Finished size: 35" x 43"*

## Supplies
### for a 35" x 43" quilt

| Fabrics | Key | Yardage |
|---|---|---|
| House | H | ½ |
| Eaves | E | ¼ |
| Chimney | C | ¼ |
| Window frames | | |
|   inner | K | ⅓ |
|   outer | M | ⅓ |
| Path | L | ⅛ |
| Shrubs | D | ⅓ |
| Step and | | |
|   chimney pots | X | ⅛ |
| Sky | S | ⅔ |
| Trim | T | ¼ |
| Window panes | D | ⅓ |
| Trees | Ba | ⅓ |
| | Bb | ⅓ |
| | Bc | ⅓ |
| Flower bed | F | ⅛ |
| Grass | G | ⅓ |
| Roof and | | |
|   inner border | R | ½ |
| Outer border, binding | | ¾ |
| Backing | | 1½" (39" x 47") |
| Batting | | 39" x 47" |
| Freezer paper | | 2 |

## PATTERN PREPARATION

1. From the pull-out pattern, trace the seven unit patterns on foundation material, transferring all numbers, letters, and markings. (We like to use white freezer paper. It is easy to see through for tracing, and it will adhere to fabric when ironed gently.)

2. With colored pencils or markers, mark matching points on seam lines where units will be joined together to ensure accurate matching of units (see photo for foundation piecing on page 91).

3. Trace the window units separately first. As each window is sewn, position it in its marked place.

4. Make a separate swatch chart as a sewing reference by placing a swatch of fabric beside the corresponding letter.

## SEWING

Refer to the Foundation Piecing instructions, pages 91–92, for general directions. Make all the windows first, then sew them into each section following the numerical order.

### Windows

The dashed lines for the windows in the pull-out pattern are the outside dimensions for the windows. There is an inner frame that surrounds each window pane, both horizontally and vertically. This frame could be considered the leading as in leaded glass windows. Then an outer frame is placed around each window. If there is more than one window in a unit, the outer frame goes between each window and around the entire unit. Some of the windows are not made with straight horizontal and vertical lines because that particular part of the house is at an angle, so perspective has changed.

Note: For the window units only, use a ⅛" seam allowance.

1. Cut strips ¾" wide for the window panes (fabric W).

2. Cut strips ⅜" wide for the inner frame (fabric K).

3. Sew one strip of fabric W to either side of fabric K. Cut the strips into segments ¾" wide (Fig. 16, next page).

Photo 7–2. Windows with inner and outer frames

4. Add one strip of fabric K to one end of the segment and join another window segment on the other side of the inner frame (Fig. 17).

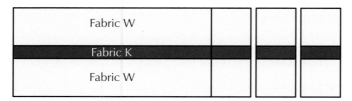

| Fabric W | | | |
| --- | --- | --- | --- |
| Fabric K | | | |
| Fabric W | | | |

Fig. 16. Strip piecing windows.

Fig. 17. Join window panes with inner frames.

5. Add another window segment if needed. Some of the windows have panes set 2 x 2, some have 2 x 3. Follow the pull-out pattern and the quilt photo to make the correct number and types of windows. When the window panes have been constructed, add the inner frame strips to the sides, tops, and bottoms of the windows. Make all the window units before starting the construction of the house. Windows are very time consuming. Be sure to take a couple of coffee breaks!

6. Once the window units (panes and inner frames) are done, add the outer frames. These strips are cut ⅝" wide (continue to use a ⅛" seam allowance). The outer frames are joined to the window units first on the top and bottom, then on the sides of the window units (Fig. 18).

You may find the window units are not quite the same size as the patterns given. (We all sew with slight variations in measurement and seam allowances.) Because each window is surrounded by "house" fabric, you can move the seam that joins the house fabric to the window slightly to compensate for any variation.

Fig. 18. Add the outer frames.

## House Construction

Construct each house section, including the windows, by following the numerical sewing order. Refer to your swatch chart for fabric placement.

Once all the sections have been completed, join them in units, then sew the units together in the following order:

### Unit 1:
Join D and H.
Add I, then B
Join F and C.
Add G to F and C.

Join D/H/I/B to F/C/G.
Join E and A.
Add E/A to complete Unit 1.

## Unit 2:
Join L and SS.
Add M and K to L/SS.
Add J.
Join Q, N, and P.
Add Q/N/P to unit.
Add Z to complete Unit 2.

## Unit 3:
Join R and S.
Join X and Y and add piece E along the side.
Join R/S and X/Y.
Add PP.
Add AA to complete Unit 3.

## Unit 4:
Join T and TT.
Add U to complete Unit 4.
Join Units 3 and 4, add to Unit 2.

## Unit 5:
Join CC and DD.
Join BB and SS.
Add KK to BB/SS.
Add CC/DD to BB/KK.
Add NN, QQ, and EE to complete Unit 5.

Join Unit 5 to Unit 2/3/4.
Add Unit 1

## Unit 6:
Join JJ and RR.
Add LL to JJ/RR.
Join HH and II.
Add HH/II to JJ/RR/LL.
Add fabric E to top of joined sections.
Join FF and GG.
Add FF/GG to sewn units to complete Unit 6.

## Unit 7:
Add Unit 7 (Section MM) to complete Victorian Manor.

## QUILT ASSEMBLY

### Borders

For the inner border, cut two strips each 1" x 26" and two strips each 1" x 34½". Add the shorter strips to the sides of the house unit and the longer strips to the top and bottom.

For the outer border, cut four 4½" strips across the width of the fabric. Join to the inner border and miter the corners if desired.

Once the borders are added, remove the foundation papers. This is a good time to rent a video and sit with a pair of tweezers!

### Finishing

Sandwich the top, batting, and binding. Quilt as desired. We chose to machine quilt in the ditch for most of the quilt because the design is quite complex and really just needs some definition. Make and apply binding as shown in General Quiltmaking Techniques (page 94). Add a hanging sleeve and label.

# Thimbleville

*We shape our dwellings,*
*and afterwards our dwellings shape us.*

*Winston Churchill*

We've created an unusual little village with a lot of room for variation. Using our "grid-graph" method with squares and half-square triangles (page 76), construction is easy and you can choose to move the buildings around to create other layouts.

*THIMBLEVILLE by Susan Purney-Mark*
*Finished size: 55" x 64"*

Quilted Havens – Susan Purney-Mark and Daphne Greig

## Supplies
### for a 55" x 64" quilt*

| Fabrics | Yardage |
| --- | --- |
| Inner Border | ⅓ |
| Outer Border | 1¾ |
| Binding | ½ |
| Backing | 3½ (59" x 68") |
| Batting | 59" x 68" |

For other pieces, see "Fabrics" section below.

*Yardage is for a quilt made with 2" squares.

The exciting part of this project is choosing the size of the squares (and ultimately your quilt). You can make 1" squares for a mini quilt, up to 2" squares or larger for a lap quilt or bed quilt. See the chart below for the different sizes you could use.

We strongly urge you to use a design wall for Thimbleville so you can see the entire piece while you are working. The design wall can be as simple as flannel sheets tacked to a piece of plywood. Make the design area as large as practical. If you need to put the work away while it's still in progress, pin the squares down and roll up the sheet. When you come back to it, the squares won't have shifted out of place. Once you've worked with a design wall, you'll wonder how you ever lived without it.

## FABRICS

One-quarter to one-third of a yard of fabric will be adequate for most large areas. Doors, windows, chimneys, etc., will require only scraps. Make a fabric swatch chart by gluing swatches to a piece of paper. Label the swatches with their location, for example, door, window, church. This reference will be handy while you are creating your quilt.

## CUTTING AND SEWING

1. There are 36 rows of 30 squares in this quilt. Using the photo and the quilt layout, determine how many squares and half-square triangles you will need from each fabric. You can work by rows or by logical sections, planning a house or a group of trees or a background section.

2. Cut selected fabrics into squares (2" for this quilt), and place them in piles for easy access while composing your design.

3. For the half-square triangles, cut squares ⅞" larger than the finished square size. For this quilt, the 2" squares will finish 1½". Therefore, you will need to start with 2⅜" squares for the half–square triangles. Mark a diagonal line on the wrong side of the lighter colored square and pin, right sides together with the other square. Sew ¼" away on each side of the drawn line. Cut along the line and press (Fig. 19). Trim, if needed, to the correct size. Make the number of half-square triangles needed for the project.

4. Follow the quilt layout on page 49 for placing the prepared squares. We like to work from top to bottom, completing each row before starting the next row.

5. You may prefer to make the quilt in sections, particularly if sewing and work

*Fig. 19. Stitch ¼" each side of drawn diagonal line. Cut on marked line to make two half-square triangles.*

| Choose square size | | | | |
| --- | --- | --- | --- | --- |
| Finished size | 1" squares | 1½" squares | 2" squares | 2½" squares |
| Quilt size (without borders) | 15" x 18" | 30" x 36 | 45" x 54" | 60" x 72 |

space are limited. To do this, mark the design in quarters and complete each quarter separately, then join quarters together to complete the top.

6. Once the design has been organized on your design wall, the sewing is done by joining the squares together in rows. Working from the lower-left corner, take the bottom squares in the first two columns and place them on a large flat surface, such as a cookie tray. Take the next two squares in the columns and place them on the previous squares, overlapping them slightly. Continue in this manner until you have moved the first two columns to the tray.

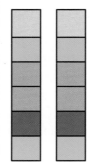

7. Take pairs of squares to the sewing machine and join them, right sides together. To chain piece the squares, do not remove each pair from the sewing machine. Slide the next two squares under the needle and continue to chain sew until all the pairs have been sewn this way. You will have a long chain of "little flags"!

8. Sew the flags into a column by joining pairs of squares with a horizontal seam. Continue joining until you have sewn all the squares into a column.

9. Press and pin this column back in place on your design wall. Repeat these steps until all the squares have been joined in columns. Press the horizontal seams of each column in opposite directions for ease in joining.

10. Sew the columns together to complete the design.

## BORDERS

For the inner borders, cut strips 1½" wide (selvage to selvage) and piece to match the measurements of the quilt. Sew the strips to the sides first and then to the top and bottom.

For the outer borders, cut 4½"-wide strips (parallel to the selvages) to the proper lengths. Sew these strips to the sides first, and then to the top and bottom.

## FINISHING

Sandwich the top, batting, and backing. Quilt as desired. You can make a free-form cable by sewing around the border in a random wavy line. Repeat four times (three times looks sparse, and five times is too crowded), attempting to reach different areas of the border with each "sweep." Make and apply binding as shown in General Quiltmaking Techniques (page 94). Add a hanging sleeve and label.

*THIMBLEVILLE MINIATURE by Joyce Newman*

Quilted Havens – Susan Purney-Mark and Daphne Greig

*Quilt layout*

Quilted Havens – Susan Purney-Mark and Daphne Greig

# Gnome Homes

*I remember, I remember,*
*The house where I was born,*
*The little window where the sun*
*Came peeping in at morn.*

Thomas Hood

Any elf or sprite would be glad to call this village home. It's a perfect way to use up scraps and little bits and pieces for embellishment. Try some silk ribbon, beads, and buttons to add the extra touches that personalize your "hobbit houses."

*GNOME HOMES by Cindy Hultsch*
*Finished size: 31" x 45"*

## Supplies
### For a 31" x 45" quilt

| Fabrics | Yardage |
|---|---|
| Sky | ¾ |
| Grass | ¼ |
| Border and binding | 1 |
| Backing | 1½ (35" x 49") |
| Batting | 35" x 49" |

Use small scraps for appliqué and corner blocks. Look for a variety of scale and texture. Try small prints and fabrics with mottled or fine lines.

## CUTTING AND SEWING

1. Cut the sky fabric 17" by the width of the fabric.

2. Cut the grass fabric 6" by the width of the fabric.

3. Sew the grass and sky fabrics together on one long side.

## APPLIQUÉ

Read General Quilting Techniques (page 88), for appliqué instructions and choose the method that best suits you. Refer to the pattern when arranging your appliqué pieces. Remember to place the background pieces first and then work toward the foreground, placing and stitching as you go. We like to pin a tear-away stabilizer to the back of the work for machine stitching appliqué. The stabilizer gives a better appearance to the stitching, and it is torn away after the piece is finished. If you are doing hand appliqué, add a scant ¼" seam allowance to all the appliqué pieces. If you are

using the fusible web method, trace the shapes without adding a seam allowance.

Most of the appliqué shapes are designed to be interchangeable. You can move the houses around to different locations or switch doors and windows from one house to another. You can make a small wallhanging with just one house and add a simple border. You can also quilt the floral border design instead of using appliqué. There is a great deal of flexibility for personal choice in how you approach this design.

Add embroidery and embellishments at this point, if desired. However, we think buttons and beads are best added during the quilting stage, because they provide an extra dimension when stitched through the layers. Trim the finished sky/grass piece to measure 22½" x 36½".

## CORNER BLOCKS

Corner blocks should measure 5" unfinished. For continuity, use fabrics in the blocks that you have used in the houses and trees. Trace the templates on the wrong side of the fabrics, lay out the pieces and, while referring to the block diagrams, sew any diagonal seams. Join the units together along the vertical seams and then along the horizontal seams.

### Friendship Star

| Fabric | Cut |
|---|---|
| Light | 4 A, 4 B |
| Dark | 4 A, 1 B |

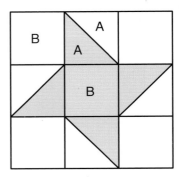

## Pinwheel

| Fabric | Cut |
|--------|-----|
| Light | 4 C |
| Dark | 4 C |

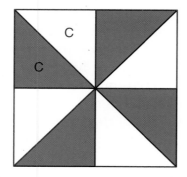

## Nine Patch

| Fabric | Cut |
|--------|-----|
| Light | 4 B |
| Dark | 5 B |

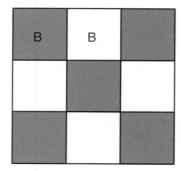

## Monkey Wrench

| Fabric | Cut |
|--------|-----|
| Light | 4 A, 1 B, 4 D |
| Dark | 4 A, 4 D |

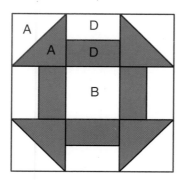

### Cutting Instructions

| Patches | Shape | Size |
|---------|-------|------|
| A | triangle | 2⅜" x 2⅜" |
| B | square | 2" x 2" |
| C | triangle | 3⅛" x 3⅛" |
| D | rectangle | 1¼" x 2" |

## QUILT ASSEMBLY

### Borders

1. Cut two strips 5" x 22½" and two strips 5" x 36½".

2. Sew a 5" x 22½" border to each side of the center piece.

3. Add a corner block to each end of the 5" x 36½" strips.

4. Sew these strips to the top and bottom to finish the quilt top.

### Border Appliqué

Mark your border for appliqué placement, or for quilting if you are not adding appliqué. Read the following information for tips on appliquéing bias stems, then proceed with placing and stitching the flowers and vines.

This is the quickest and neatest method of bias-strip appliqué that we know, and it works well for any length or width of bias.

1. Cut bias strips 1½" wide. Join strips together if necessary for length. Fold in half lengthwise, wrong sides together; press.

2. Pin strips along placement lines marked on the background and stitch ⅛" from the raw edges (Fig. 20).

3. Turn the pressed fold of the strip over the raw edges and slip stitch in place (Fig. 21). Try this method with different widths of strips so you can have a variety of bias strips for different purposes.

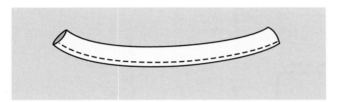

*Fig. 20. Sew to background with ⅛" allowances.*

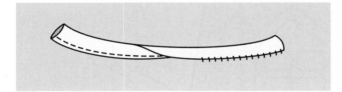

*Fig. 21. Fold tube over raw edge and stitch.*

## FINISHING

When appliqué has been completed, mark quilting designs. This is an opportunity to be playful – create cloud designs in the sky, tile patterns on the roofs, echo quilt the window panes. Experiment and have fun. When the quilting has been completed, make and apply binding as shown in General Quiltmaking Techniques (page 94). Add a hanging sleeve and label.

*Close-up of ribbon embroidery*

*Close-up of ribbon embroidery*

*GNOME HOMES by Susan Purney-Mark*

Enlarge pattern pieces 200% to make
a 31" x 45" quilt, or use patterns "as is"
for a smaller quilt.

Patterns may be photocopied for
personal use only.

*Border flower*

Enlarge pattern pieces 200% to make a
31" x 45" quilt, or use patterns "as is"
for a smaller quilt.

# Log Cabin Retreat

*I will arise and go now, and go to Innisfree,*
*And a small cabin build there, of clay and wattles made:*
*Nine bean-rows will I have there, a hive for the honey-bee,*
*And live alone in the bee-loud glade.*

William Butler Yeats, "The Lake Isle of Innisfree"

Three peaceful log cabins near the shore of a lake are featured in this project. Trees surround the cabins, and there are mountains in the distance. Fabric can be textured for the trees and mountains before the blocks are foundation pieced, giving the quilt an extra dimension. Directions are given for producing your own textured fabrics, if you like.

*LOG CABIN RETREAT by Daphne Greig*
*Finished size: 67" x 79"*

## Supplies
for a 67" x 79" quilt

| Fabric | Yardage |
| --- | --- |
| Water | ¼ each of 5 fabrics |
| Rocky shore | ¼ each of 4 fabrics |
| Background | 2 |
| Trees | ½ each of 5 fabrics |
| Tree trunks | ⅛ total from 1 or 2 fabrics |
| Mountains | ½ each of 4 fabrics very dark, dark, medium, medium dark |
| Sky | ½ |
| Cabins | ¼ |
| Doors | ⅛ |
| Roofs | ¼ |
| Accent border, outer border, binding | 1¼ |
| Backing | 72" x 84" |
| Batting | 72" x 84" |
| Lightweight tricot fusible interfacing | 3 |
| Foundation material | 3 (see pages 91-92 for options) |

## CUTTING

All strips are cut across the fabric, selvage to selvage. The Log Cabin, mountain, tree, and cabin blocks are foundation pieced (patterns on pages 63–64). Note that the foundation patterns given will make a 33½" x 38½" quilt. To make a 67" x 79" quilt, shown in the photo, enlarge the patterns 200 percent. If you prefer, the Log Cabin blocks can be strip pieced as described on the following page.

### Water

Fabric 1: Cut one 2" strip for the 9" Log Cabin blocks. Cut two 2½" strips for sashing.

Fabrics 2, 3, 4, and 5: Cut three 2" strips from each fabric. Set aside one strip of each of these four fabrics for the pieced borders.

### Rocky shore

Cut two 1¼" strips from each fabric for 9" Log Cabin blocks. Cut two 2" strips for pieced borders.

### Background

Cut seven 2½" strips for sashing.
Cut four 2" strips for the pieced borders. Use remaining fabric for blocks.

### Trees

Cut one 2" strip from each fabric for the pieced borders. Use remaining fabric for foundation-pieced blocks.

### Mountains

Cut one 2" strip from each fabric for the pieced borders. Use remaining fabric for foundation-pieced blocks.

Note: see Piece by Piece, Build your Home page 76, for instructions on how to manipulate fabric.

### Sky

Cut two 2½" strips for sashing. Cut two 2" strips for pieced border. Use remaining fabric for foundation-pieced blocks.

## *Accent border, outer border, and binding*

Cut fifteen 1½" strips for accent and outer borders. Use remaining fabric for the binding.

## LOG CABIN BLOCKS

Make six Log Cabin blocks to create water and a rocky shore. Blocks can be made by foundation piecing (pattern on page 64), or the 9" blocks can be strip pieced, as described below.

1. Cut six 2" squares from water fabric-1 strip for the centers of the Log Cabin blocks.

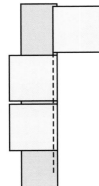

2. Place a 2" water square on a 1¼" rocky shore strip, right sides together, and sew with a ¼" seam allowance. Place another square next to the first and continue sewing. Repeat with all six center squares (Fig. 22) .

*Fig. 22. Sew squares to strip.*

3. Cut the units apart, trimming the strip even with each square. Press the seam allowances toward the rocky shore strip.

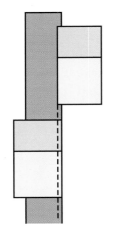

4. Place each unit on a second rocky shore strip, right sides together, with the rocky shore log at the top. Sew with a ¼" seam allowance (Fig. 23).

*Fig. 23. Sew with rocky shore log at the top.*

*Finished unit*

5. Trim the second strip even with each unit. Press seam allowances toward the rocky shore strip.

6. Place the units on the 2" water strip, right sides together, with the second rocky shore log at the top of the strip. Sew with a ¼" seam allowance (Fig. 24).

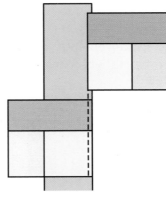

7. Trim the water strip even with each unit. Press seam allowances toward the water strip.

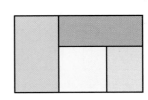

*Fig. 24. Sew units to the water strip.*

*Finished unit*

8. Continue in this manner with a second water strip, then two rocky shore strips, two water strips, two rocky shore strips, two water strips, and two rocky shore strips. Always place the last log added at the top when you sew the units to the next strip. You will have six blocks measuring 9½" (Fig. 25).

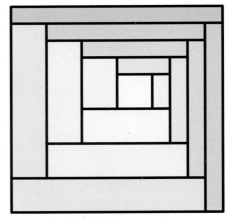

*Fig. 25. Finished Log Cabin block*

9. Sew the six blocks together in a row, as shown in the Quilt layout, page 61.

# TREES, MOUNTAINS, AND SKY

Trace 30 tree and 12 mountain blocks for foundation piecing. Refer to General Quiltmaking Techniques for foundation piecing, page 92. If you made textured fabric, use it for the trees and mountains.

## *Mountains*

1. Fig. 26 shows the color arrangements for the mountain blocks. Sew three blocks with each color arrangement.

*Fig. 26. Sew three of each.*

2. Arrange the 12 blocks in two rows, each containing six blocks (see the quilt layout on the facing page). Sew the two rows together.

*Close-up of scrunched mountains*

# CABINS

Trace three cabin blocks for foundation piecing. Prepare the cabin fabric by using one or all three of the following techniques (see Piece by Piece, Build your Home, pages 77–78, for sewing instructions for these techniques and others):

Corded pin tucking with the pin tucks on the right side of the fabric.

Corded pin tucking with the pin tucks on the wrong side of the fabric. (Use light-colored cording to simulate chinking between logs.)

Couching over a cord or yarn. (Use light-colored cord or yarn to simulate chinking between logs).

Foundation piece three cabin blocks.

Sew trees and cabins into three rows as shown in Fig. 27.

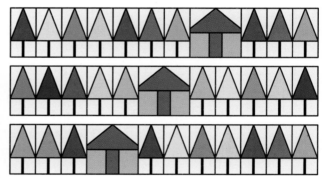

*Fig. 27. Tree and cabin rows*

# QUILT ASSEMBLY

The quilt layout on the facing page shows the arrangement of the rows of blocks and sashing strips. The sashing strips are made by piecing the 2½" strips of water, background, and sky together to make sufficient length to match the rows of blocks.

## *Accent Border*

Sew enough 1½" accent strips together, end to end, to make sufficient border lengths. Sew to each side of the quilt.

Quilted Havens – Susan Purney-Mark and Daphne Greig

*Quilt layout*

Quilted Havens – Susan Purney-Mark and Daphne Greig

## Pieced Borders

Cut the 2" border strips into random lengths, varying from 4" to 8". Arrange the strips to match the color changes in the quilt and then sew the strips together along the short ends. Sew three of these borders around the quilt, one at a time (see quilt, page 57).

## Outer Border

Sew the remaining 1½" strips together to make sufficient length to sew to each side of the quilt.

## Finishing

Layer the quilt top with batting and backing and baste well. Quilt where desired. This is a great opportunity to use free-motion quilting techniques to give added dimension to the quilt. Quilt waves in the water area, rock shapes in the rock section, and clouds in the sky. Stipple quilting with rayon thread was used in the mountain and tree shapes. Make and apply binding as shown in General Quiltmaking Techniques (page 94). Add a hanging sleeve if you plan to use this quilt as a wallhanging, and add a label.

*FLANNEL LOG CABIN RETREAT by Cindy Hultsch and Amy Andreasen*

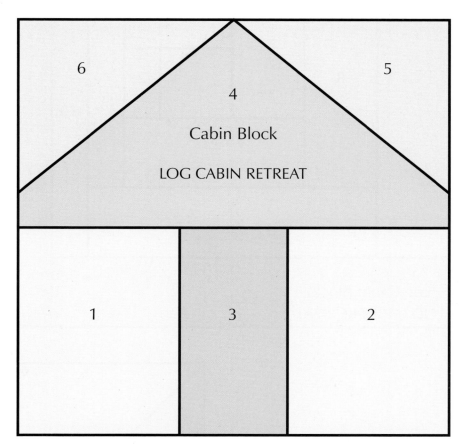

Cabin Block

LOG CABIN RETREAT

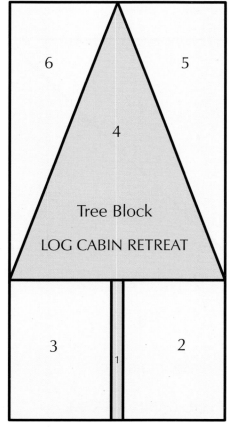

Tree Block

LOG CABIN RETREAT

Use these blocks for a
33½" x 38½" quilt.

Enlarge 200% to make 9" blocks
for a 67" x 79" quilt.

When trimming, leave ¼" seam
allowance around the outside of
each unit.

Patterns may be photocopied for
personal use only.

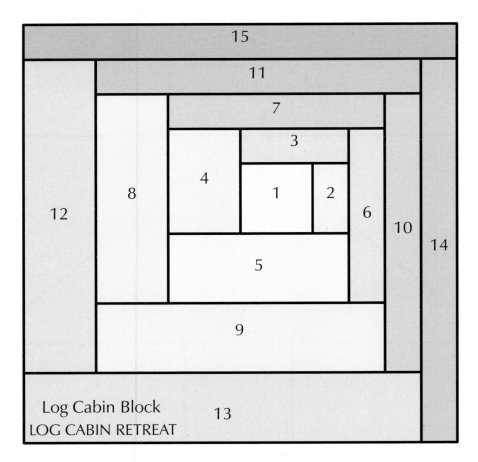

Log Cabin Block
**LOG CABIN RETREAT**

Use these blocks for a
33½" x 38½" quilt.

Enlarge 200% to make 9" blocks
for a 67" x 79" quilt.

When trimming, leave ¼" seam
allowance around the outside of
each unit.

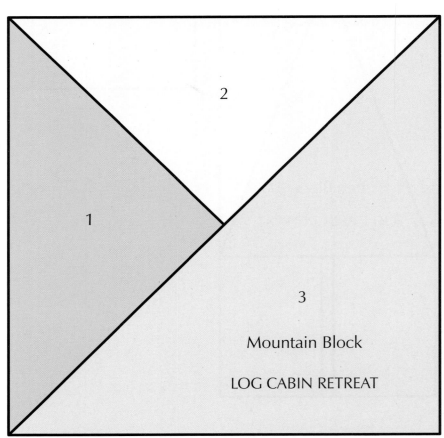

Mountain Block

**LOG CABIN RETREAT**

Quilted Havens – Susan Purney-Mark and Daphne Greig

# Hillbilly Hotel

*…and they all lived together in
a crooked little house.*

*Nursery rhyme*

You can try some really wild and funky fabrics for this wallhanging. Fusible web and folk-style appliqué make it a quick and easy project – one that children can participate in. Indeed, the whole project might be fun for a group of people.

*HILLBILLY HOTEL by Aileen Conway*
*Finished size: 32" x 24"*

## Supplies
for a 32" x 24" quilt

| Fabrics | Yardage |
| --- | --- |
| Sky | ½ |
| Ground | ⅓ |
| Houses, tree, and accents | scraps |
| Log cabin blocks lights darks | ⅛ each of four fabrics ⅛ each of four fabrics |
| Backing | 1 (36" x 28") |
| Binding | ¼ |
| Batting | 36" x 28" |
| Perle cotton in several shades | |
| Buttons and beads | |
| Fusible web | |

## CUTTING

1. Cut a rectangle of sky fabric 26" x 34". (Excess will be trimmed away before adding the Log Cabin border.)

2. Trace all appliqué units on the paper side of fusible web (for more information, see page 90.) Following manufacturer's directions, apply the web to the wrong side of the appliqué fabrics. Cut out the pieces.

## QUILT ASSEMBLY

1. Lightly mark the placement of the appliqué pieces on the background fabric.

2. Arrange the appliqué pieces, using the pattern for placement reference. Tuck the houses and tree behind the ground fabric to anchor their bases.

3. Fuse the fabrics in place, layering where needed. The folk appliqué stitching is done after the border blocks have been added. Trim the center panel to 16½" x 24½".

4. Make 24 Log Cabin blocks for the border by using the foundation-piecing instructions in General Quilt-making Techniques, page 91–92. Trim blocks to 4½". Arrange the blocks around the center panel, rotating them until you achieve a design that is pleasing to you.

5. Sew four blocks together for the borders on each side of the center panel. Then sew the borders to the panel. Repeat this step for the eight blocks for the top and bottom borders of the quilt.

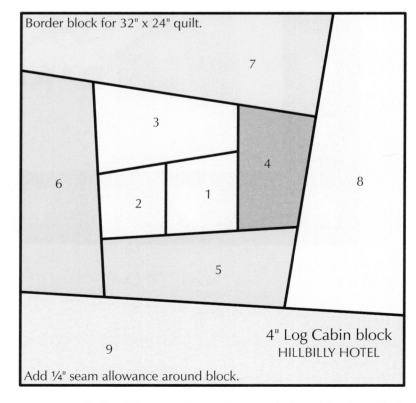

Border block for 32" x 24" quilt.

4" Log Cabin block
HILLBILLY HOTEL

Add ¼" seam allowance around block.

## FOLK APPLIQUÉ STITCHING

You can choose to do this stitching as part of the quilting process. If so, leave this part until the quilt is sandwiched together. If you choose this method, keep in mind that it will be more difficult to pull the threads through more layers, so greater care must be taken.

Use a chenille needle for stitching. It has a sharp point and a large eye for the thread. A size 22 is a useful size for many projects.

Use fairly short lengths of perle cotton (15"–18") for stitching. The thread has to go through several layers of fabric in some places, and the stress will pull fibers off the thread and fabric.

A single thickness of thread is needed. Put a small knot at the end. Start stitching on the right side of the work. (The knot is left showing.) Stitch ⅛" away from the raw edges of the appliqué pieces.

## FINISHING

Layer the quilt with the batting and backing and baste well. Quilt where desired. At this point, beads and further embellishments can be added. Make and apply binding as shown in General Quiltmaking Techniques (page 94). Add a hanging sleeve and label.

Enlarge pattern 200% to make a 32" x 24" quilt, or use patterns "as is" for a smaller quilt.

Patterns may be photocopied for personal use only.

Border block for smaller quilt.

| | | 7 | |
| 6 | 3 | 4 | 8 |
| | 2 | 1 | |
| | 5 | | |

9

2" Log Cabin block
**HILLBILLY HOTEL**

Enlarge pattern 200% to make a
32" x 24" quilt, or use patterns "as
is" for a smaller quilt.

Quilted Havens – Susan Purney-Mark and Daphne Greig

# Donation

# Dwelling

# Donation Dwelling

*However we toil, or wherever we wander,*
*our fatigued wishes still recur to home for tranquility.*

Goldsmith, *The Citizen of the World. No. 103.*

DONATION DWELLING by Rose Bates, Janet Beitz, Wendy Birch, Ann Dalgliesh, Darlene Dressler,
Jill Gardener, Daphne Greig, Julie Jackson, and Moira Sullivan
Finished size: 50" x 65"

This quilt was designed to be made by a group – any gathering of individuals who have fabric, some basic quilting skills, and a desire to help those less fortunate. The design can be copied as needed for these purposes. The quilt can be given to shelters, the Red Cross, or even raffled to make money for charitable organizations. All it takes is a commitment of time and fabric to make a difference in people's lives. So gather your friends, your neighbors, your co-workers and give a part of yourselves to others.

The instructions are written to resemble a three-act play for six individuals. Select members of your group to "play" the parts. If you're making more than one quilt at a time or you have a larger group, just assign the same part to more than one person and let them share the job.

Make one copy of the play for each participant. Ask each person to read the complete play and mark her part. Make sure each person understands the instructions.

## THE CAST

**Rotary Ruth**: Knows how to use a rotary cutter, mat, and ruler to cut squares.

**Marking Molly:** Can draw lines on fabric with a marker and ruler, and can use rotary tools.

**Sewing Susan:** Can sew ¼" seams with a sewing machine.

**Sewing Sally:** Can sew ¼" seams with a sewing machine.

**Pressing Penny:** Knows how to press.

**Patchwork Patty:** Manipulates fabric squares and acts as the director.

## THE MATERIALS

Each player brings the following supplies mentioned in the table below:

- Fabric strips are cut across the fabric selvage to selvage. Select various prints for the strips.

- Give the players guidelines for fabric colors.

- Fat quarters are approximately 18" x 22".

## THE PROPS

- Two rotary cutters, two mats, and two 6" x 24" rulers.

- One chalk marking pencil (visible on dark fabric).

| Fabric | R. Ruth | M. Molly | S. Susan | S. Sally | P. Penny | P. Patty | Total |
|---|---|---|---|---|---|---|---|
| Blue print strips 5½" wide | 3 | 3 | 3 | | | | 9 |
| Red print strips 5½" wide | 2 | 2 | 2 | 2 | | | 8 |
| Green print 5½" squares | 5 | 5 | 5 | 5 | | | 20 |
| Blue print Fat quarter | 1 | | | | | | 1 |
| Brown print Fat quarter | | 1 | | | | | 1 |
| Yellow print Fat quarter | | | | 1 | | | 1 |
| Batting | | | | | 55" x 70" | | |
| Backing | | | | | | 55" x 70" | |
| Tying thread (Perle cotton) | | | 1 spool | | | | |

- Two sewing machines with neutral thread (a shade of gray is best).

- One iron and ironing board.

## *Act I*

The Players gather and set up the workspace, talking among themselves.

**Rotary Ruth:** Lays out cutting tools, layers eight blue print strips in pairs, right sides together, passes to Sewing Susan. Ruth cuts six 5½" squares from the ninth blue print strip, and passes to Patchwork Patty.

**Marking Molly:** Lays out cutting tools, sets aside three red print strips for binding, layers four of the remaining red print strips in pairs, right sides together, and passes layered strips to Sewing Susan. Molly cuts two squares 5½" from the eighth red print strip; passes to Patchwork Patty.

Cuts door from yellow print fat quarter, 10½" x 15½"; passes to Patchwork Patty.

**Sewing Susan:** Sews pairs of strips together on one long edge with a ¼" seam allowance; passes to Pressing Penny as each set is finished.

**Pressing Penny:** Presses seams of pairs of strips in one direction; passes to Rotary Ruth and Marking Molly.

**Patchwork Patty:** Arranges the 20 green print squares in two rows in a pleasing way for the grass (Fig. 28); passes them to Sewing Sally. Directs the action as each player completes her part.

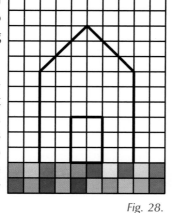

*Fig. 28.*

**Sewing Sally:** Sews the two rows of 10 green squares together with ¼" seam allowances and passes to Pressing Penny.

## *Scene 2*

**Rotary Ruth:** Cuts three 5⅞" squares from the blue print fat quarter; passes to Marking Molly.

Cuts six 5½" squares and three 5⅞" squares from brown print fat quarter; passes 5½" squares to Patchwork Patty and 5⅞" squares to Marking Molly.

**Marking Molly:** Marks a diagonal line on the wrong side of the blue print 5⅞" squares and marks again ¼" from each side of the line.

Layers these squares with brown print 5⅞" squares, right sides together, and passes to Sewing Sally.

**Sewing Sally:** Sews pairs of 5⅞" squares along outer diagonal lines, and passes to Patchwork Patty.

**Patchwork Patty:** Cuts sewn 5⅞" squares along center diagonal line; passes to Pressing Penny.

Arranges six brown print 5½" squares to begin roof formation (Fig. 29).

Places two red print squares above door (Fig. 30, facing page). Arranges six blue print 5½" squares for the sky (Fig. 31, facing page).

**Pressing Penny:** Continues pressing the seam allowances of pairs of strips in one direction. Passes to Rotary Ruth and Marking Molly.

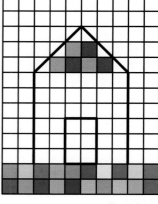

*Fig. 29.*

Presses half-square triangles toward brown print. Passes to Patchwork Patty.

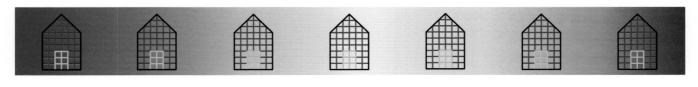

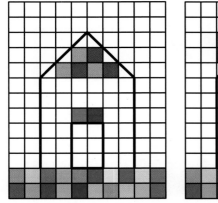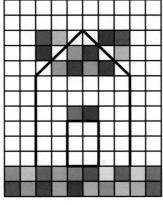

Fig. 30.　　　　　　Fig. 31.

Presses seam allowances of row of green print squares in one direction. Passes to Patchwork Patty.

**Rotary Ruth and Marking Molly:** Cuts pairs of strips in 5½" segments. Pass to Patchwork Patty.

**Patchwork Patty:** Trims "ears" from half-square triangles and arranges brown/blue print half-squares for roof.

**ALL:** Gather with Patchwork Patty and, referring to photo on page 70, arrange the rest of the pieces to complete the quilt top.

## FIRST INTERMISSION

(This is a good time for coffee and cookies!)

### Act II

The players have finalized the layout for the pieces that form the quilt top. Sewing Susan, Sewing Sally, and Pressing Penny are stationed by their equipment. Each has a partner for this scene:

**Rotary Ruth** works with **Sewing Susan**.
**Marking Molly** works with **Sewing Sally**.
**Patchwork Patty** works with **Pressing Penny**.

.

**Rotary Ruth:** Begins with top row of quilt, aligns pieces; passes to Sewing Susan. Passes sewn sections to Pressing Penny.

**Marking Molly:** Begins with bottom row of quilt, aligns pieces, and passes to Sewing Sally. Passes sewn sections to Pressing Penny.

**Sewing Susan and Sewing Sally:** Sew sections.

**Pressing Penny:** Presses sections.

**Patchwork Patty:** Takes pressed sections and places them in quilt layout. This process continues until the whole quilt top has been sewn together.

## SECOND INTERMISSION

(More coffee and cookies!)

### Act III

The players gather the backing, batting, tools, and materials for their favorite basting and tying methods.

**ALL:** Layer the backing (right side down), batting, and quilt top (right side up) and baste together.

Tie the quilt with double knots.

**Patchwork Patty:** Prepares a label for the back of the quilt and has each person sign it.

**Rotary Ruth:** Cuts six 2½" strips from the three red print strips set aside for binding.

**Sewing Susan:** Joins binding strips together to make enough binding to go around the quilt.

**Pressing Penny:** Presses the binding in half lengthwise, wrong sides together.

**Sewing Sally:** Sews the binding to the quilt using a ¼" seam allowance.

**Marking Molly:** Trims the backing and batting even with the binding.

**Patchwork Patty:** Turns the binding to the wrong side and slip stitches by hand; sews the label on the back.

**ALL:** Take a bow and deliver your quilt to its new home.

### THE END

# Piece by Piece

Quilted Havens – Susan Purney-Mark and Daphne Greig

We hope you enjoy making the projects we've included in this book, but these houses probably don't look like the one you live in. Here are some techniques to successfully depict your own home in fabric.

## CONVERTING A PHOTOGRAPH

Take a really good look at your house. Go across the street to get some distance away. What elements are you most proud of? Is it the front porch that you love so much? The welcoming front door, the style of windows, the garden? These are the details that you will want to give prominence in your project. Move around to get different perspectives. You may notice something you don't want to depict, depending on your viewing angle.

Take several photographs of your house. First, take pictures of the full house from the angle you like best. Then take some detailed closer shots of the elements you want to incorporate. Have the film developed. Take the full house photograph to a photocopier. Enlarge the photograph 200%. Use standard 8½" x 11" paper. Make at least two copies.

### Simplify the Design

Look at the close-up photographs. What elements do you want to emphasize? What details do you want to hide or change? In my case, I don't want to see that funny row of trees across the front of my house. I really like the divided windows in our house, and the siding is a nice feature. The gutters and downspouts add nothing to the design, so I'll leave them out. Mark one copy of your design with these decisions. Cross off what you don't like, circle the things you do like, and add or move trees or shrubs. Don't worry about how you will make the elements yet. We'll have lots of ideas for that later in the chapter.

Place a piece of tracing paper over the marked copy of your house. Trace only the elements you want to

*Daphne Greig's house. Mark design decisions on photograph.*

include in your quilt. This will be your master plan. Enlarge the traced design with a photocopier until it is the size you want your project. You may have to tape pages together as you enlarge and enlarge again. When you are happy with the size and design, make two final copies. Use one copy for actual-size templates for your quilt.

*Trace elements of house design.*

Now is the time to decide which technique or techniques you will use for your quilt. It's not necessary to limit yourself to one technique. Consider combining one or more to achieve the effects you want. Each technique has particular advantages. For example, foundation piecing allows you to have small details and odd angles. Appliqué can be used for three-dimensional shapes. Strip piecing is useful for seminole work, borders, and quick piecing. Have a look at the project chapters and pull ideas from them as well.

## GRID-GRAPH METHOD

This method was used for the houses in Thimbleville. It is quick to do and can be as simple or as detailed as you choose to make it.

Once your design is finalized, trace your house on a clear plastic sheet with a grid of four squares to the inch. You will have to move some angles so they intersect at the lines on the grid. You may want to turn all diagonal lines into 45-degree angles so piecing will be easier. You can still piece other angles within a square, but cutting them out with templates may be the easiest and most accurate approach. Remember that you can put almost any shape within a square as long as the piece will measure the same as the other squares for sewing.

When the drawing on the grid is finalized, go over your markings with a fine-point permanent marker to make clear lines.

Next, use colored pencils or markers to color in the squares. Refer to your photograph for color placement and shading. Remember that the size of your quilt will be determined by the cut size of the fabric squares and the number of squares you used in your design.

## DECISION-MAKING TIME

There are many techniques for making the parts of your house more realistic. Fabric can be manipulated or the surface embellished to resemble actual construction materials. We suggest you read the rest of this chapter, making notes on the particular techniques that might apply to your project. The list in the next column was used for my house.

## FABRIC MANIPULATION

### Scrunching

This technique makes three-dimensional fabric that can add extra texture, particularly for trees, shrubs,

| Decision List for Daphne's house | |
|---|---|
| **TECHNIQUE** | **WHEN TO USE** |
| Scrunching | not applicable |
| Pin tucking | use for siding |
| Couching threads | mutton bars of windows |
| Folded inserts | roof edges, window frames |
| Shark's teeth | not for my project |
| Photo transfer | maybe my family in a window? |
| Stamping, stenciling, painting | not this time, but maybe if I can't find the right sky I could paint one? |
| Buttons, beads, and baubles | not applicable |
| Yo-yos | layered to make shrubs under the window |
| Ribbon embroidery | flower garden |

and roofs. Work with approximately ½ yard. Thoroughly wet the fabric and gather it into a tight ball. Use elastic bands to hold it. Put the ball in the dryer and remove it when it is dry. This may take several drying cycles.

Remove the elastic bands. Open the ball of fabric and gently arrange it, right side up, on your ironing board until it is a wrinkly rectangle, approximately 15" x 35".

Using steam and the cotton setting, press with an up and down motion of your iron. Do not slide the iron along the fabric, press down, then lift the iron and move it to another section.

Gently turn the fabric over so the wrong side is up. Place a 14" x 34" piece of lightweight tricot fusible interfacing on the wrong side of the fabric and fuse by using the manufacturer's directions. Again, don't slide the iron. You want to keep the wrinkles.

*Scrunched fabric, front side*

*Scrunched fabric, wrong side*

Turn the fabric to the right side again and press to ensure a good bond with the interfacing.

This scrunched fabric can be used wherever texture is desired, such as for trees, mountains, and house roofs.

## Pin Tucking

Pin tucking is a natural choice for creating siding or clapboards. It can also be used to add dimension to roofs. Pin tucks require some special accessories for your sewing machine. First you will need a twin needle. This accessory is two needles that work at the same time. They can be fairly close together or wider apart. Refer to the manual for your machine to find the largest width you can use on your machine. You also will need a pin–tucking foot. This foot has grooves underneath. (The number varies from three to nine.) Feet with fewer grooves will make deeper pin tucks. Again, refer to your manual or talk to your sewing machine dealer to find the appropriate foot for your machine.

Since you have two needles for this technique, you will need two spools of thread, one for each needle. You may have to thread your machine in a particular way to accommodate the two threads. Check your manual.

As you sew, the two top threads make two rows of stitches, close together. The single bobbin thread travels from one thread to the other and a tuck is created on the right side. The depth of the tuck is determined by the width of your twin needle and the number of grooves on the foot.

## Corded Pin Tucks

You can also add extra dimension to your tucks by running a cord under the work between the two rows of stitching. The cord will fill the tuck, making it more defined.

Usually the right side of the work (the one with the tucks) is used to add dimension. The wrong side can be just as effective if you make corded pin tucks. This technique can be used to create the chinking in one of the cabins in the Log Cabin Retreat quilt. The pin tucks were sewn on the wrong side of the fabric and a cord was used underneath the tucks (on the right side of the fabric). The bobbin thread color matches the cord.

*Corded pin tucks were used to simulate siding and roofing.*

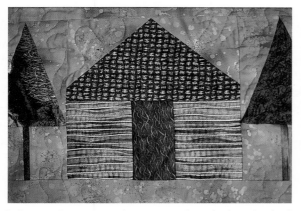

*Corded pin tucks, wrong side, were used as chinking for the logs.*

## Couching Threads

This technique is simple to do. You just need a variety of weights of thread or yarn, invisible sewing thread, and a zigzag sewing machine. The threads are sewn to the fabric by sewing over them with a zigzag stitch using invisible thread. There are sewing machine feet available to help keep the couching threads in the center of the foot as you sew. These are particularly useful if you are creating curves with the threads. Practice this technique with different threads or thread combinations and select colors that are most appropriate for the design element you are

*Couching threads used for window mullions and vines.*

creating. This technique is used to make mullions in windows and to create a vine creeping along a wall.

## Three-Dimensional Appliqué

Additional texture can be added to your design by creating three-dimensional elements that stand out from the body of the project. This technique can be used effectively in the Gingerbread House project (page 31). When making this quilt with cotton fabric rather than felt, the roof scallops and roof edging can be lined to create a three-dimensional effect.

To achieve this look, add a ¼" seam allowance to the pattern piece and cut two pieces from the fabric. Layer the pieces, right sides together, and sew with a ¼" seam allowance and a small stitch length. Leave an opening for turning. Trim all seam allowances to ⅛", turn right side out, and press. Slip stitch the opening closed. Do not sew all the edges down to the base fabric. Leave some edges free so they stand out from the project. The project chapters give details on which edges to leave free.

Ruching has enjoyed a revival in popularity. Consider using it for flowers in a garden or as embellishment in a border.

## Folded Inserts

Inserts (flat piping) can be used to define edges of roofs or window frames. Cut narrow strips 1" wide by the length required. Fold the strip in half lengthwise, wrong sides together, and include it when you sew the seam (matching the raw edges). This width will result in a ¼" flat piping.

## Shark's Teeth

Shark's teeth, as a decorative element, are most commonly used to embellish clothing. However, they make wonderful roofs because they are full of texture and visually interesting.

*Shark's teeth*

Use a piece of fabric 2" wider than the finished measurement you need and 2½ times the finished length. Select a thread that matches the fabric closely or use invisible thread. You will also need a marking pencil. Test to be sure the marks can be removed later.

Measure 2" from the bottom edge of a piece of fabric and draw a horizontal line. Measure 2¼" from this line and mark another line. Continue marking lines 2¼" apart. Stop marking at least 2" from the top edge. Be sure to keep the lines parallel. These are the fold lines.

Now mark the stitching lines. Measure ¾" above the first line you drew and mark a line. Mark a stitching line ¾" above each fold line (Fig. 32).

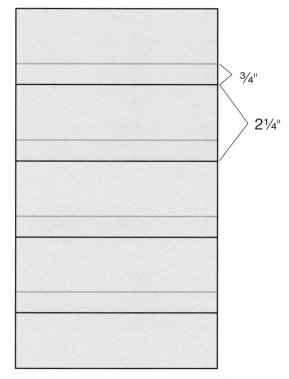

¾"

2¼"

*Fig. 32. Mark fold lines 2¼" apart. Mark sewing lines ¾" from fold lines.*

Set your machine to sew a short stitch length. Carefully fold the fabric on the first fold line, press in the fold, and sew along the first stitching line. Lightly press the tuck toward the bottom to keep it out of the way. Fold on the second fold line, press, and sew on the second stitching line. Again press the tuck toward the bottom. Continue until all stitching lines are sewn. Now press all the tucks toward the bottom. Press well. The piece should be very flat.

Next, mark cutting lines on the tucks. Place your ruler vertically on the right side of the tucked fabric. Mark a line at the beginning of each odd-numbered row. Measure ¾" from these first marks and mark a line on each even-numbered row. Measure ¾" from these marks and mark the odd-numbered rows again. You

should have marks 1½" apart along each row and the rows will be staggered (Fig. 33).

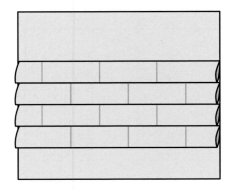

*Fig. 33. Mark vertical lines every 1½" in staggered rows.*

Cut only one row at a time. Starting with the bottom row, use small sharp scissors to snip the tuck at every vertical line (just to, but not through, the stitching line). Finger press the cut edges to meet the stitching line, forming a triangle. The folded edges should meet at the center of the triangle. Use your iron to press each triangle in place (Fig 34).

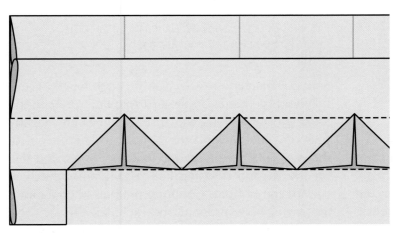

*Fig. 34. (Detail) Cut on the vertical lines and fold to form triangles.*

From the top side of the tuck, stitch close to the original stitching line, catching the raw edges of the tucks (Fig. 35). Repeat these steps for each row.

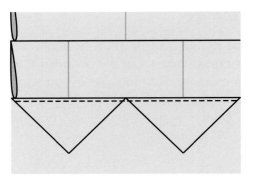

*Fig. 35. (Detail) Stitch in place.*

## SURFACE DESIGN

### *Photo Transfer*

Photo transfer techniques give quilters perfect opportunities to include special photos in their quilts. Imagine a face or two in the window, personalized labels or special trim, porticoes, shutters, or other images. There are a number of ways to make photo transfers. Check with your local quilt shop for special transfer papers. These usually need to be taken to a copy center to have the images transferred to the paper. You can then take the paper and transfer the images to your fabric with an iron. Some copy centers have the ability to transfer directly to fabric. Check the facilities in your area.

Technology marches forward and there is so much that is useful to quilters. We are now able to use our computers to print directly on fabric, with reliable, consistent results. This method gives us the opportunity to design our own fabric with house or architectural images. We can also search the Internet for useful images and change them by distorting, rotating, flipping, or otherwise introducing our own ideas before applying them to fabric. We can be guaranteed that there will always be something to challenge us to try new ways and methods for our quilting.

*Photo transfers on THE ROAD TO A FRIEND'S HOUSE IS NEVER FAR by Jean Avison and friends.*

ers' directions for their use. Generally, they will need to be heat-set with an iron to make them permanent.

*Stenciling on OUR HOME AND NATIVE LAND by Daphne Greig.*

## Stamping, Stenciling, and Painting

Fabric isn't the only medium you can use in your house projects. Paints and inks can add extra interest in many ways. There is a huge selection of stamps and stencils available in craft and specialty shops. Have a good browse through them and you're sure to find some that are perfect for your projects. Consider using them in borders to complement a theme or enhance a quilting design. You could paint areas to replace an appliqué and create shadows.

It is possible to create your own stamps from sponges, leaves, and cut-up shapes. Stencils are easy to make with plastic template material or discarded x-ray film. Inks and paints can be purchased that are specifically designed for use on fabric. Follow the manufactur-

## EMBELLISHMENTS

### Cross-stitch

Cross-stitch is an embellishment that can be appropriate for a house quilt. It could be as simple as a little quilt on a clothesline. Use cross-stitch in combination with a canvas base. Create a more complex design incorporating trees, flowers, and features from the houses, such as windows, doors, or gingerbread trim.

*Cross-stitch on PEGGY'S HOUSE by Peggy Estey and Susan Purney-Mark.*

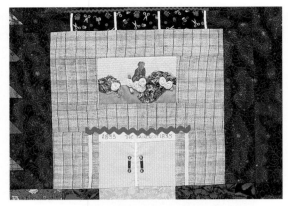

*Embellishments on* THE ROAD TO A FRIEND'S HOUSE IS NEVER FAR *by Jean Avison and friends.*

## Buttons, Beads, and Baubles

You can have so much fun using these treasures as embellishments for your quilt. Spend some time collecting and searching through craft and bead shops and check out the junk jewelry in the bottom of your dresser drawer. Flea markets and thrift shops are good sources, too.

Be creative. Think of letters and numbers for your houses, kittens in the windows, and stars in the sky.

Have beading needles and beading thread on hand. Embellishments can be applied as you go or as part of the quilting process.

## Lace

There is a lovely shop near us, which we visit whenever we're in need of inspiration. They carry a wide selection of lace and ribbons, which are perfect for gingerbread trim on a house, curtains in the window, or background motifs for flowers.

If you can find cotton lace and trim, it can be painted or dyed to blend with your fabric selections. Sometimes, colored lace or lace with colored threads is available.

If you are making a quilt to commemorate an anniversary, wedding, or special event, make it even more memorable by including fabric or lace from a wedding dress, christening gown, or similar important article. If you are making such articles, remember to save the scraps of leftover fabrics so they can be used for "memory" quilts or something equally special.

*Lace curtains in* DEBBIE'S HOUSE.

## Embroidery

Embroidery has long been a popular addition to quilting. It can be as simple as lettering, or it can lead to some of the lovely work seen in the best quilt shows.

DEBBIE'S HOUSE *by Debbie Whitfield and Susan Purney-Mark*

*Embroidery on GINGERBREAD HOUSE by Joanne Manzer.*

*Yo-yos on HOUSE AROUND THE CORNER MINIATURE by Amy Andreasen.*

There are many products suitable for use with your houses. Silk ribbon is available in myriad colors. Consider, also, using the variegated shades in flowers, stems, and leaves.

*Silk ribbons on GINGERBREAD HOUSE by Joanne Manzer.*

Embroidery floss used in combination with silk ribbon and beads will provide a rich "flower bed" for your home. Best of all, these gardens never need weeding!

## Yo-yos

While these little "critters" have been around a long while, yo-yos really are a useful addition for embellishment. We have used them as smoke from the chimney in the "Gnome Homes," but consider making them as tiny hollyhock flowers or enlarging them for appliqué.

## Other Thoughts

Some of the quilts you have seen in this book are the result of a friendship exchange of blocks within one of our quilting groups. You might like to present a new neighbor with a little quilt with a block depicting her new home. Consider, too, a gift for a friend leaving the area. It would be a memento of the friends she is leaving behind. One of our friends has done an exquisite rendition of her husband's office in an historic downtown building. A school class could make a project of portraying buildings in the community.

We've had fun thinking of some of the possibilities open to you in creating your home. There are so many more, limited only by imagination. Create and build your homes and send us pictures!

# General

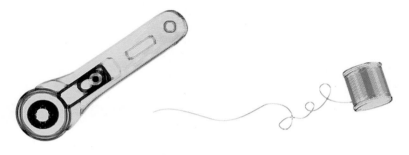

**TECHNIQUES**

# Quiltmaking

Quilted Havens – Susan Purney-Mark and Daphne Greig

## FABRIC CHOICES

There are spectacular fabrics on the market designed for "house builders" – bricks and stones for chimneys and pathways, wood grains for walls, all sorts of textures for roofs. The choices for gardens surrounding your houses are limitless. Floral fabrics can add so much to your designs. They can be used "as is" in the blocks to portray gardens, or cut out and appliquéd in place. Consider floral fabrics as a base for embellishment with silk ribbon, beads, or quilting. Don't forget to look at the reverse side of fabrics.

They often have surprising elements you may not see on the right side but which can improve your project.

Start collecting interesting fabrics whenever you visit quilt shops. For many projects, you will need only ¼ yard or even less. Quilters can never have enough fabric, and your "stash" is just like a pantry cupboard. It always needs replenishing!

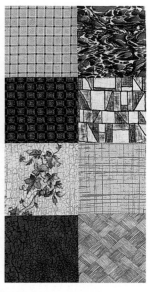

Whatever design you choose, it is recommended that you buy top quality 100% cotton fabric. Just as a builder must select the best materials for a real house, so must you. The extra expense will be obvious in the quality of the work you do.

## ROTARY CUTTING

Rotary-cutting tools have revolutionized quiltmaking for many quilters. Quilters love the accuracy and speed provided by these tools. Rotary-cut quilts go together better because the individual pieces are exact. We can cut many pieces at once so we get to the "fun" part sooner!

There are many styles of cutters, rulers, and mats on the market. Again, purchase quality tools that will last. Select a cutter that feels comfortable in your hand. Select rulers that are clearly marked in ⅛" increments. Be sure the markings are visible on both light and dark fabrics. Select a mat that is large enough to lay out a piece of fabric folded once selvage to selvage. You may want a smaller mat for special cutting techniques, such as cutting around templates.

### Rotary Cutter Safety

Always cut away from yourself and use the blade cover whenever you are not cutting. Store your rotary cutter safely out of the reach of children and pets. Use a sharp blade, because many accidents occur when a dull or nicked blade is forced to cut. Dispose of blades by wrapping them in paper and tape before tossing in the trash.

## THREADS

For the general piecing of the projects, we used a 100% cotton thread. We prefer a silk finish thread in size 50/3. This thread has been a reliable mainstay in our sewing room for many years. A light gray color can be used for most seams. If you are using mostly dark fabrics, you may wish to use a darker gray. Buy the largest spools you can, so you're ready when inspiration hits.

### Embroidery Threads

The machine-appliqué projects in this book were made with machine embroidery thread. Our first choice is a 100% cotton in size 60/2. It is a finer thread, which, when used in a satin stitch, gives a lovely soft sheen and seems to lie flatter than regular sewing thread. You may also consider using some of the wonderful fancy threads available. If your quilt shop doesn't carry them, check out the needlework or sewing machine dealers. They can also be a wealth of information for instruction on using the

threads in your machine, which needles are best for the threads you use, machine settings, and much more.

Rayon and metallic threads come in a rich array of colors, including variegated shades, which could add interesting detail to your work. Use these threads judiciously. The idea of embellishment is to add interest, not to detract from the overall appearance.

### Silk Thread

If you haven't discovered the wonderful advantages of silk thread, now would be a good time to try some. Silk thread is perfect for hand appliqué, and although it is available in a wide range of colors, we

like to use the neutral shades of gray or taupe. The thread is quite fine, and when used in hand appliqué, it buries itself between the fabric threads and almost disappears. Keep the thread length quite short; 15"–18" is a good length.

### Needles

We can't stress enough how important a sharp needle is in achieving good results in your work. If you can't remember the last time you replaced your needle, this is the time to do it. Remember "the right tool for the right job" in choosing your needles. Having a ready supply of spares can cut down on frustration and emergency trips to the quilt shop.

For general purposes, we use a jeans/denim 80/12 needle. It has a fine but strong shaft with a good size eye. With metallic and specialty threads, use a metallic needle. It has a Teflon-coated eye, which reduces friction and heat buildup on your threads.

## USING TEMPLATES

Templates can be made with any sturdy material – cardboard is one choice, but it is easier to use plastic that is designed for templates. You can see through the plastic to accurately trace templates and to transfer any markings, such as piece number and grain line. The plastic can be easily cut with scissors. Template plastic is available with or without grid lines. The plastic without grid lines is best for tracing templates from this book. Use the gridded template plastic when you are drafting your own blocks. Use

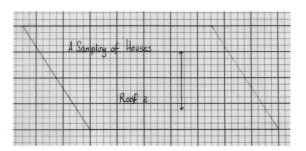

*Pattern drafted on gridded template plastic.*

a fine point permanent marker to trace templates. Transfer all information from the original, including the block name and size, template number (or letter), and the grain line. Store your templates in zipper-style plastic bags with the name of the block written on the outside.

The templates in this book do not have seam allowances added. We find it easier to trace around a template on the sewing line and to "eyeball" a ¼" seam allowance when we cut the pieces out of fabric. That way, the exact sewing lines are marked and your seams will be precise.

Trace templates on the fabrics with a very sharp pencil. Sharpen the pencil frequently to maintain accuracy. Don't forget to add the ¼" seam allowances when you cut the fabric pieces.

## PRESSING

A good relationship with your iron will produce reliable, consistent results. As you sew, press each seam while it is closed to stabilize the threads and the fabric. Then open the pieces and press again, generally pushing the seam allowances to the darker side. For some of our projects, other pressing instructions are given so that seam allowances will lie flat in subsequent sewing. Remember to press with an up and down motion, not pushing the iron across the fabrics. Pushing the iron will distort the shapes of pieces, and measurements will be inaccurate.

## MACHINE SEWING

Many projects can be made by using a simple sewing machine that sews straight, even stitches. For other projects, a machine with more features will be valuable. The main skill you will need is the ability to sew an accurate ¼" seam allowance. Many machines have special feet available that are exactly ¼" wide. The needle position can be moved on some machines so you can maintain accurate ¼" seams.

Take the time to sew several seams and check that they are exactly ¼". This time will pay off in the end.

To sew anything other than a straight stitch, refer to your owner's manual for the specific selections available. Generally, the selections will include stitch selection, stitch width, and stitch length. When you are using a new stitch, test it first and note the best settings for the project you are doing. (Don't be afraid to write in that manual – it's yours!)

A well-tuned sewing machine is a pleasure to use. Clean your machine regularly, referring to your owner's manual for instructions. Consult a trained service person if your machine needs more than regular cleaning. They are specially trained to keep your machine in top condition.

## APPLIQUÉ

There are many excellent books on the various methods of appliqué. We are including our favorites, but we encourage you to use your preferred style. However, do read through the instructions thoroughly to be certain the method you choose is suitable for the project. Time may also be a factor.

## HAND APPLIQUÉ

### *Freezer Paper*

Quilters are masters at finding useful products outside of the quilting realm, and freezer paper is one of the best examples. Here in Canada, our supermarkets and butcher shops carry only the brown paper, so any visit to the United States means a visit not only to the quilt shops but also the grocery store. Fortunately, our quilt shops now stock white freezer paper, which we prefer. Freezer paper has a poly-coated back which, when pressed with a dry iron on a medium setting, will adhere to fabric. The paper is easy to remove once the stitching is done.

For the freezer-paper method, trace the appliqué shapes on the paper side, cut along the line, and iron on the wrong side of the fabric. Cut out the fabric pieces, adding a ³⁄₁₆" turn-under allowance all around by eye.

Turn the allowance to the wrong side and press the fold. Gently apply small dabs of fabric glue to hold the allowance in place. Clip the allowance where necessary so it will lie flat (see photo below). The edge of the freezer paper will give a nice firm edge to your hand appliqué.

Pay careful attention to the placement diagrams in the chapters so the sequence in which you appliqué

*Wrong side of appliqué shape with clipped allowance.*

is correct. This is especially important when layering appliqué pieces on top of one another.

Some of the pieces may be too small for using freezer paper easily. In this case, we hand baste the turn-under allowances to the wrong side. If you leave your knot on the right side of the fabric, you can snip it and remove the basting thread after the piece is appliquéd in place.

Once an appliqué piece is stitched down, cut away the background from the wrong side, leaving ¼" of the background next to the appliqué stitching line. You can then easily remove the freezer paper from the wrong side of the piece.

## Folk Appliqué

This is a fun "rough and ready" quick method of appliqué that gives some great texture. Use a perle cotton #5 or some decorative thread of a similar weight. Stay away from knobby or textured threads because they are too difficult to pull through the fabric layers. Chenille needles are perfect for folk appliqué because they have a large eye for the heavier threads and a sharp point for piercing the fabric.

You can choose to use this method at the quilting stage, sewing through the three layers of top, batting, and backing. It will be a little more difficult to stitch through all three layers, so take extra time and care for this.

*Detail of folk appliqué, HILLBILLY HOTEL by Aileen Conway*

Apply your appliqué pieces, using fusible web according to manufacturer's directions. Use a single strand of thread and knot the end. Start from the front of the work (leaving the knot on top gives a "funky" touch) and take small running stitches. Place the stitching line about ⅛" from the raw edge of the fabric. Gauge the stitch length to the area you are

working, shortening it slightly if you need to turn a corner or return to your starting point. Finish off by taking the thread to the back of the work and taking a couple of small stitches that do not show on the front.

*Detail of HILLBILLY HOTEL by Kathy Black*

*Detail of folk appliqué, HILLBILLY HOTEL by Kathy Black*

## MACHINE APPLIQUÉ

### Fusible Web

We have used fusible web on some of our machine appliqué projects. It is a great product that speeds the process considerably. Buy the best quality you

can find. We prefer a web that has a paper backing on both sides. Once fused to the back of the appliqué pieces, it will adhere to the background, but you can move it around while deciding on the final placement. Once the design is completed, a final pressing will fuse it in place.

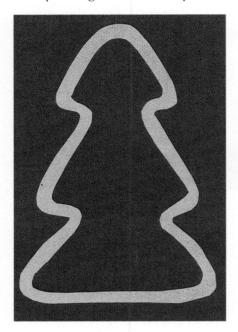

*Close-up of "skeleton" cut from fusible web.*

If you don't care for the firmer "hand" of fusible web, consider using it only around the outside edges of the appliqué piece. Cut out the entire shape of the appliqué from fusible web and then trim away the inner portion, leaving a ¼" "skeleton" around the outside. Fuse the trimmed web to the back of the appliqué piece in the normal manner.

## Satin Stitch

To finish the edges of the appliqué shapes you have fused in place, sew a smooth, even satin stitch with your sewing machine. A satin stitch is a zigzag with the stitches very close together, but not so close that the machine has trouble advancing. Test various settings of stitch width and length on your sewing machine until you are happy with the results. We recommend a 2-mm stitch width, and you may find that loosening the upper thread tension slightly will

give your satin stitch a smoother appearance. Use machine embroidery thread for best results.

To clearly see where to sew, use an open-toe embroidery foot or a clear plastic one. Check with your machine dealer for recommendations. Position your appliqué to the left of the presser foot. The stitches should just cover the edge of the appliqué shape. For

smoother results, place a stabilizer underneath the work as you sew (tearaway stabilizer, tracing paper, etc.). Sew several stitches with 0 width at the beginning and end to lock your stitches.

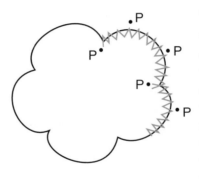

To ensure smooth curves when you appliqué by machine, you will have to stop and turn your work as you sew. It is important that your needle remains in the fabric when you lift the presser foot to turn your work. Use the "needle down" option if your machine has one. It is also important that the needle is in the correct position when you turn your work. These are the pivot points. The figure shows potential pivot points (P).

## Buttonhole (or Blanket) Stitch

Buttonhole stitching by machine is another option for finishing the edges of fused appliqué shapes. An open-toed embroidery or clear plastic foot helps you see where to sew. Test your machine settings first. Your stitches should not be too close together or too far apart. The machine must feed evenly and not bunch up, and there should not be too much space between the horizontal stitches. Regular weight

**Quilted Havens – Susan Purney-Mark and Daphne Greig**

sewing thread gives this stitch more definition, but it can also be done with rayon thread for a shiny look.

The straight part of the stitch (the portion of the stitch that travels along the edge of the appliqué) should be on the right with the appliqué piece on the left. If your machine sews the stitch the other way, you can probably "mirror image" the stitch to change it to this configuration. Stitch width should be between 2 and 2.5 mm. To sew curves and turn corners, be sure your needle is in the work on the outside edge (straight part of the stitch) before you lift the presser foot to pivot.

### Free-Stitch Appliqué

This method combines fusible web with straight-stitch appliqué. The fabric edges are left unfinished, and the stitching is very close (⅛" or less) to the edges. Use a regular stitch length with machine embroidery, or similar lightweight thread, to closely match the fabric. Stitch over the design at least three times, running the stitching lines right beside, rather than on top of, one another. Pay attention to the placement sequence of the appliqué pieces. Some will be fused and stitched before others are added.

*Close-up of free-stitch appliqué in GNOME HOMES by Susan Purney-Mark*

Chimneys are placed before the roofs and windows, and so on. Working from the background to the fore-ground is a good guideline to follow.

## FOUNDATION PIECING

Foundation piecing, as its name implies, is piecing on a foundation. The foundation can be tracing paper, plain newsprint, photocopy paper, or products specifically designed for the technique. We have also found that the examination-table paper used by doctors is a great product for foundation piecing. The original master design must be transferred to the foundation material. This can be done by photo-copying if your foundation can be used in a copier, or it can be done by tracing. If you are tracing, use a ruler and a sharp pencil.

Make the number of copies required in the quilt instructions. Transfer all lines, numbers, and letters to your copies.

When the project is divided into several units that need to be joined together, mark points on each foundation piece for easy matching.

If a block has unusual angles and many pieces that make it difficult to tell which fabric goes where, we recommend making one extra copy of the block pat-tern. Write your fabric choices on this extra copy and then cut it apart on the lines. Use these pieces to rough cut the sections for your block. To rough cut, place each paper piece right side up on the wrong side of the appropriate fabric. Cut approximately

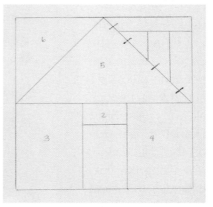

*Matching points marked on foundaion pieces*

½" around the outside of the piece. Hint: To cut multiples of the pieces for more than one block, be sure to layer the fabrics wrong side up.

Rough cut all the fabric pieces for the block before you begin piecing. You can store them in small zipper-style plastic bags until you are ready to sew.

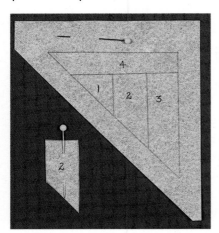

### Sewing

Set the machine stitch length to 15–20 stitches per inch (1.5 on most machines). Small stitches make it easier to remove the foundation material after the block has been constructed because the needle creates perforations for tearing.

1. Select the fabric for section #1. Place it right side up on the wrong side of the foundation so it extends over the lines of area #1 at least ¼" on all sides. You can use a glue stick or pin to lightly secure the piece in place.

2. Place piece #2 over piece #1, right sides together, lining up the edges near the line between pieces #1 and #2. Pin through all layers for stability. From the right side of the foundation, sew along the line, extending the stitching ⅛" beyond the line. Turn the foun-

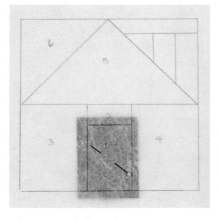

*Placement of piece #1*

dation over and trim the allowance to ¼". Flip piece #2 to the right side, finger press, and pin in place.

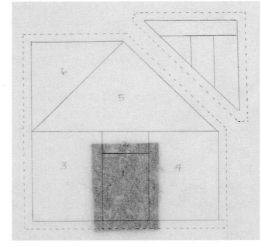

*Piece #2 sewn to piece #1*

3. Select the fabric for the remaining sections and follow the same procedure in numerical order. Press after each addition and remove pins when necessary.

4. Press the block carefully after the last section is sewn in place. Trim the block with your rotary cutter, ruler, and mat, making sure you leave a ¼" allowance around all sides of the block.

5. Carefully remove the foundation material from the block. Tweezers are a great tool for removing the paper.

*Finished block, right side*

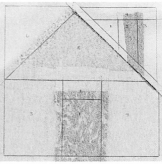

*Wrong side*

# QUILT FINISHING

## Marking

It is best to mark your quilt design on the completed quilt top before layering. There are many good marking products on the market. Keep in mind that marks must be visible for the quilting process and easy to remove afterward. Ask friends and quilting teachers for their recommendations and test several to find the ones you like best.

## Batting

Choosing batting for projects can be a confusing process because there are so many available to us. Simply put, your choice should depend on the size of the project, whether you are hand or machine quilting, and how you are going to use the quilt.

Polyester battings are lighter in weight, generally have a higher loft, and are easy to quilt. Cotton and cotton-blend battings are firmer, have a lovely drape to them, and may be a little more difficult to hand quilt. Our batting of choice is an 80% cotton and 20% polyester blend, which is easy to hand or machine quilt, has a good weight for both wallhangings and quilts, and is simple to clean.

## Sandwiching

Good preparation for the quilting process will ensure an even, straight quilt with no puckers or wrinkles. When you are sandwiching a quilt, have a large work surface, preferably at table height. Often, your local quilt shop is willing to let you use classroom tables for this process. When there are a few quilts to sandwich and baste, many quilters gather some friends, put on a pot of coffee, and make a social time of it.

1. Lay the backing, wrong side up. Smooth out any wrinkles and tape the fabric to the table in the corners and at frequent intervals.

2. Lay the batting on next, smoothing it out from the center to the edges. If the batting has been in a plastic bag, air it out beforehand to let it fluff up and eliminate creases.

3. Add the quilt top right side up and smooth it from the center outward. Make sure at each stage that there is enough of the backing and batting all around the outside edges. Two inches is a good rule of thumb.

4. Pin or thread baste, starting from the center outward in a starburst fashion. There should be no more than 4"–6" between threads or pins.

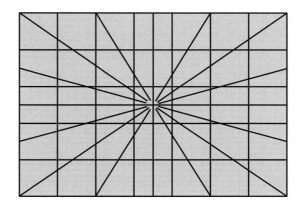

## Quilting

Your quilting choices are many, and most often the quilt design will suggest some possibilities. Time considerations and quilting method used will also guide your decisions.

Remember to use products you are comfortable with and take time to enjoy the process.

## Tying

If you don't have time to quilt, you can tie the layers of your quilt together. Select a batting that doesn't require close quilting lines, and sandwich the layers

together as usual. We recommend perle cotton and a sharp needle for tying. To prevent the knotted threads from tearing the quilt when it is used and washed, tie the knots at seam intersections for added strength. From the right side of the quilt, push the threaded needle down through all the layers, leaving a 4" tail of thread on the top. Make a stitch about ⅛" wide and bring the thread to the top. Cut the thread, leaving a second 4" tail of thread. Tie the threads into a square knot close to the surface of the quilt. Trim the thread ends evenly to about ½".

## Binding

Binding is the final step in completing your quilt. A well-finished edge is one in which the binding lies flat, there is no puckering along the borders, and the edge is even all the way around the quilt.

The binding can be straight cut, that is, cut from selvage to selvage, or it can be cut at a 45-degree angle to the edge of the fabric, which will provide a true bias. The necessity of a bias binding is evident when your quilt edge is curved. Bias binding will stretch gently around the curves and lie flat when stitched. Straight-cut binding serves the purpose when your quilt edges are straight.

For our wallhangings we have cut the binding 1½" wide. If you are making a bed or lap quilt, then we recommend a binding cut 2¼" wide. Fold the binding in half, wrong sides together. The double thickness provides better wear and a good firm edge.

To determine the length of binding needed, measure the perimeter of the quilt and add 15". To reduce the bulk when sewing the lengths together, cut the ends of the strips at a 45-degree angle, sew these seams together, and press them open (Figs. 36a–c). Press under a scant ¼" along one side if your binding is cut 1½". This will provide a finished edge to turn to the back and slip stitch down. If you are using 2¼" strips,

*Fig. 36a. Cut the ends of strips at a 45-degree angle.*

*Fig. 36b. Stitch ends together.*

*Fig. 36c. Press open.*

press the binding in half. Turn in and press one 45-degree end to make a nice finished edge.

Pin the binding along one side of the quilt. Begin sewing near the middle of the side. Leaving about 8" of the beginning end of the binding unsewn, stitch along the binding and stop ¼" from the first corner. Backstitch (Fig. 37). Slide the quilt from under the presser foot.

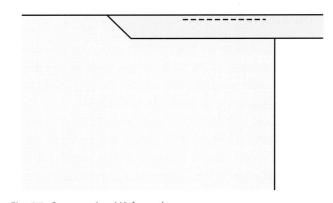

*Fig. 37. Stop sewing ¼" from the corner.*

Fold the binding up and away from the quilt, making a 45-degree angle. Then fold it back down, aligning

the binding with the next edge of quilt (Fig. 38). Pin the binding to the next side.

Begin sewing the next side ¼" from the corner and end ¼" from the next corner. Continue these steps until you are approximately 10" away from the starting point. Trim any excess binding, leaving approximately ½" to overlap with the beginning edge. Make this cut at a 45-degree angle. Tuck this end inside the loose binding at the beginning and continue sewing the remaining binding to the quilt.

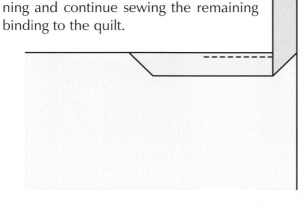

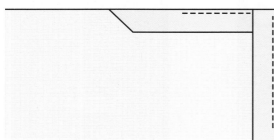

*Fig. 38. Align the binding with the next edge.*

Remove the quilt from the machine. Leaving ¼" all around, trim the excess batting and backing from the edge, being careful not to cut into the binding. Trim the corners of the batting and backing at a 45-degree angle to reduce the bulk in the corners. Turn the binding to the back and slip stitch it along the machine stitching line, making a miter at each corner.

## DISPLAYING YOUR QUILT

If your quilt is designed to be displayed on a wall, the best way is to add a hanging sleeve. Cut a piece of muslin (or extra backing fabric) that measures 8" wide by the width of the quilt. Finish the two short edges by folding ¼" to the wrong side twice and sewing. Fold the strip in half, wrong sides together and sew the raw edges with a ½" seam. Press the seam allowance open; flatten tube and center open seam.

Pin the sleeve to the quilt back, just below the binding at the top edge, centering it along the width. Slip stitch the top edge of the sleeve in place securely. Push the bottom edge of the tube up a bit (the tube shouldn't lie quite flat) and pin the bottom edge in place. Again, slip stitch the edge securely.

Insert a dowel or decorative rod, and hang the quilt, supporting the ends on brackets. If the quilt is particularly wide or heavy, you may need to add additional support in the center. If this is the case, the hanging sleeve should be in two or more sections. The space between the sections will allow for the additional bracket.

## TAKING CREDIT

The final step in creating your masterpiece is to attach a label with the quilt's title, and your name, address, and date. It's an important record for yourself to keep track of your work and your progression as a quiltmaker. As well, it provides future generations with information about us and the ways we lived and quilted.

Your label can be as simple as a rectangle of muslin with your name and the date printed with a permanent marker, or it can be a work of art in itself. Use hand or machine embroidery, draw motifs to match the quilt's design, or use stencils to embellish the label. If the quilt is a gift, you may want to record who the quilt is for and the occasion. Finish the edges of the label and slip stitch it in place to the back of your quilt.

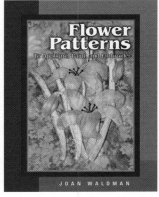

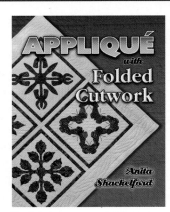
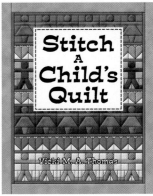

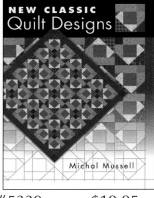
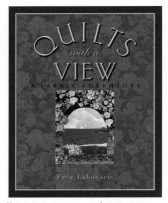
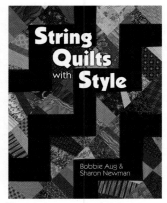
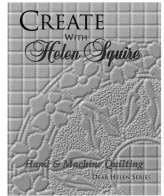